PSYCHOTHERAPY WITH THE ORTHODOX JEW

Herbert Strean, D.S.W.

JASON ARONSON INC.
Northvale, New Jersey
London

Production Editor: Judith D. Cohen

This book was set in 11 point Palacio by Lind Graphics of Upper Saddle River, New Jersey, and printed and bound by Haddon Craftsmen of Scranton, Pennsylvania.

Copyright © 1994 by Jason Aronson Inc.

10 9 8 7 6 5 4 3 2 1

Library of Congress Cataloging-in-Publication Data

Strean, Herbert S.
    Psychotherapy with the Orthodox Jew / Herbert Strean
        p. cm.
    Includes bibliographical references.
    ISBN 1-56821-230-5
    1. Psychotherapy — Religious aspects — Judaism — Case studies.
    2. Psychotherapy patients — Religious life — Case studies.   3. Judaism and psychoanalysis — Case studies.   4. Judaism and psychology — Case studies.   5. Orthodox Judaism — Psychology — Case studies.   I. Title.
    BM538.P68S77   1994
    616.89′14′088296 — dc20   94-2461

Manufactured in the United States of America. Jason Aronson Inc. offers books and cassettes. For information and catalog write to Jason Aronson Inc., 230 Livingston Street, Northvale, New Jersey 07647.

To Rachel Pearson Strean, in memoriam

"Her ways are ways of pleasantness, and all her paths are peace."

Proverbs 3:17

Contents

Introduction

The relationship between psychodynamic psychotherapy and religion has been frequently tempestuous and consistently ambivalent. To this day, many psychotherapists identify with Freud's position on religion. The founder of modern psychotherapy was a militant atheist and in his book *The Future of an Illusion* (1927), Freud took the position that religion would someday yield to rationality, the way a symptom is eradicated when it is thoroughly analyzed. In fact, Freud considered religion to be the universal obsessional neurosis—something irrational, infantile, an expression of deep conflict, and devoid of sensibility.

Although the majority of clinicians who have written on religion, such as Greenson (Nemiroff et al., 1992), have referred to religious faith as "weak, fragile, and magical" and prayer as a form of servile obedience bordering on masochism, there are a number of psychotherapists (e.g., Bergmann 1982, Ostow 1982) who have pointed out how religious identity can strengthen the ego and bolster the ego ideal.

Because religion is a controversial issue for many therapists, when it comes up in the treatment situation it arouses strong countertransference reactions. At a recent panel discussion, "The Significance of Religious Themes and Fantasies During Psychoanalysis," chaired by Lee Grossman (1993), Jacob Arlow commented that many clinicians try to explain to patients the irrational nature of religion; or, at the opposite extreme, they regard religion as a private domain, to be kept apart from psychotherapeutic investigation. Arlow had to implore well-trained and experienced psychoanalysts to treat religious thoughts and experiences the same neutral way they respond to other clinical data and not attempt to validate or invalidate the religious philosophy of the patient.

The difficulties that psychotherapy has had in coping with and understanding religious behavior very much mirror Freud's strong ambivalence toward his own religion, Judaism. Although an avowed atheist, Freud was an active member of B'nai B'rith, spoke and wrote frequently on Jewish subjects, was enamored of Moses and identified strongly with him, married an Orthodox Jewish woman, and declared he would always remain a Jew. Freud, concerned over psychoanalysis's vulnerability to attack as the "Jewish science," thought Jung could be a much-valued successor to him as the leader of psychoanalysis because he was not Jewish. Yet, he also told Karl Abraham that Jung could not understand psychoanalytic phenomena too well because it took a Jewish mind to do so (Jones 1953–1957, Meghnagi 1993).

The ambivalent attitude of dynamic psychotherapy toward religion, starting with Freud and continuing to the present, has been matched by religion's ambivalence toward psychotherapy. The Reverend Oskar Pfister, a friend of Freud's and an ardent supporter of psychoanalysis, often berated Freud and other analysts for not embracing religious concepts and making them a part of psychoanalytic theory (Ostow 1982). Until quite recently many clergymen forbade their parishioners to become patients of psychotherapists and averred that discussing sexual and aggressive fantasies with a therapist was sacrilegious.

Yet, Dr. Smiley Blanton, a psychiatrist and an analysand of Freud's, founded the Institute of Religion and Psychiatry, and many pastoral counselors continue to incorporate psychodynamic concepts into their therapeutic work. The well-known contemporary Freudian psychoanalyst Dr. William Meissner is a practicing Catholic priest.

As religion becomes more secularized—a phenomenon noted in all contemporary religions (Smith and Handelman 1990, Malony and Spilka 1991)—and as psychotherapists become more disciplined and humane, a greater number of devoutly religious individuals are entering psychotherapy as patients. Furthermore, many of them are finding they can be helped therapeutically without fearing they are betraying or compromising their religious ideals and principles. As Stanley Leavy (1993) stated in concluding his review of Malony and Spilka's (1991) book, *Religion in Psychodynamic Perspective: The Contributions of Paul W. Preyser,* " . . . the ignorance of psychoanalysts on matters of religion is only equaled by the ignorance of psychoanalysis on the part of the faithful" (p. 488).

During the past fifteen years I have noted in my own practice as well as in the practices of clinicians I supervise or teach, a growing number of religious leaders (priests, ministers, and rabbis) as well as large numbers of devout followers of major religions entering therapy and using it well. I have particularly been impressed with the large numbers of Orthodox Jews who have sought therapeutic help from me or my students, colleagues, or supervisees.

Inasmuch as I have treated or supervised the therapy of nearly 100 Orthodox Jewish patients during the last decade and a half, I am now in a position to discuss in depth and breadth some of their unique dynamics and responses to the therapeutic situation. For example, I have found that just about every Orthodox Jew who becomes a patient in psychotherapy is in a struggle with his or her God. I have learned that almost every Orthodox Jew who has come into treatment has conflicts about observing many of the Jewish rituals, for example, praying, observing the Sabbath, keeping a kosher diet, and heeding admonitions about sexual practices. I have also noted in my own practice and in those I supervise that an Orthodox Jew, although usually an active and curious learner, often has a great deal of difficulty learning from the therapist and demeans and castigates him or her for long periods of time. In addition, I have been very impressed that some of the strongest countertransference reactions take place in therapists, Jewish and non-Jewish, when they treat Orthodox Jewish patients (Grossman 1993, Meghnagi 1993).

It is the aforementioned issues, among others, that I will pursue in depth and breadth in this book. In Chapter 1, "A Psychodynamic View of Orthodox Judaism," I will attempt to explain the psychodynamic meaning of such issues as allegiance to God, who, although referred to as a King of the Universe and a protective father, is also experienced as a nurturing mother. I will also discuss the obsessive-compulsive features of the many Jewish rituals and consider why orality is a prominent feature of Jewish life. The many gender problems inherent in Orthodox Judaism will also be reviewed, including a dynamic explanation of what every Orthodox Jewish man says on awakening each morning, "Thank God I am not a woman!"

Other features of Orthodox Jewish life that will be assessed in Chapter 1 are the emphasis on learning (Jews call themselves "people of the book"), a preoccupation with success, elitism, and being "a light unto the nations" (Jews refer to themselves as "God's chosen people"), and a powerful concern with superego commands, particularly with "sin."

In Chapters 2 to 6 I will discuss four Orthodox Jewish patients who were in intensive psychotherapy with me over an extended period of time. Although names and other identifying data will be altered to protect confidentiality, the cases will reveal the genuine struggles of the patients, particularly around their Orthodoxy. The discussion of the patients will also indicate their idiosyncratic responses to the treatment situation. In addition, I will reveal some of my prominent countertransference responses to my patients and evaluate how these reactions helped or hindered therapeutic progress.

Chapter 2 will feature "The Ambivalent Rabbi." Rabbi Cohen came to treatment because he had sexual and interpersonal problems with his wife, and severe problems relating to his 7-year-old son. Although revered by his congregants and colleagues, he was frequently depressed, had problems with his self-esteem, and was not sure he wanted to continue being a rabbi. In discussing Rabbi Cohen's interpersonal and intrapsychic problems, I will highlight the patient's dramatic fight with his God and demonstrate its similarity to his struggles with his parents. I will also show that when Rabbi Cohen began to question his God as well as other features of Orthodox

Jewish practice, he became extremely negativistic toward therapy and toward me. In this chapter I will focus sharply on the transference–countertransference relationship and present many examples of our responses to each other. Prominent in this patient's dynamics was a latent homosexuality, which was defended by a pervasive arrogance and contemptuousness. I will show that as these dynamics were analyzed and as Rabbi Cohen's hatred toward family and others diminished, he could move toward "a more flexible" practice of Judaism.

"The Masochistic Rebbitzin" will be the subject of Chapter 3. A 34-year-old woman, the wife of a rabbi, Rachel Abramowitz came into treatment because she had severe psychosomatic problems. In social situations, which necessarily were many, her heart beat rapidly, she blushed profusely, and she became alternately nauseated, constipated, or had diarrhea. In addition, Rachel often stammered or stuttered in social situations. Most of these symptoms appeared soon after she married Rabbi Nathan Abramowitz.

In her therapy, Rachel slowly and with much pain became aware of how much she hated being her husband's "servant." Her demeaned position in marriage, however, was a continuation of her inferior status as a girl, sister, and daughter in her original family "where boys were everything and I was a nobody."

Although Rachel began to feel better and function at a higher level after she could accept some of her repressed rage, she modified her early positive view of the therapist and then saw him as "a manipulator" and "a seducer" who did not have her "best interests" in mind. In many ways, I reminded her of her "arrogant" father (an Orthodox Jew who was a cantor) and of her husband who acted "too smugly."

The intense negative transference of Rachel Abramo-

witz will be discussed in depth, and of course my own
frustrations, irritations, and the individuals in my past
with whom I identified Rachel will also be discussed and
analyzed. When Rachel could emotionally perceive that
she wanted "to continue a war with Jewish men" and
could take some responsibility for her own "wars," she
became much more assertive at home and in the synagogue, liked herself more, and became less of a servile
masochist. She began to see herself less as a rabbi's wife
and more as a woman who enjoyed loving and working.

Chapter 4 will discuss the dynamics and treatment of
Meyer Stein, a 29-year-old "Born-Again Orthodox Jew"
(*Ba'al Teshuva*). Meyer was a single man who had moved
from job to job, girlfriend to girlfriend, and therapist to
therapist. Anxious, depressed, lonely, sexually impotent,
and self-loathing, Meyer was referred to me by his physician because he also suffered from migraine headaches,
asthma, and other psychosomatic ailments.

I was Meyer's fifth therapist, and almost as soon as he
initiated therapy with me he began to question its value
and validity. He had recently become an Orthodox Jew,
and because he was quite sure I wasn't, he concluded that
I was a "second-class citizen." Meyer was quite convinced
my values, ethics, and philosophy of life were question-
able and he repeatedly told me that I was "untrust-
worthy."

It took Meyer a long time to see that the battle in which
he was engaged with me was the same futile one he
maintained with parents, siblings, colleagues, girlfriends,
and others. It took him an even longer time to recognize
that he was using his Jewish Orthodoxy as a defense
against much castration anxiety and that by exhibiting his
religious identity to everyone he was trying to put down
others and artificially make himself feel more potent.

As Meyer eventually saw that I would not argue with

him nor oppose his modus vivendi, his deep yearning for love slowly began to emerge. Eventually he recognized that his Orthodoxy not only defended against his inner uncertainties but was a way of trying to locate a loving family. When the psychological truth about Meyer's religious preoccupations emerged in his therapy, he became less involved with prosletyzing and more interested in having constructive relationships with people.

The last patient to be discussed, in Chapter 5, is Joyce Kaplansky, an ardent feminist. Thirty-one years old and single, Joyce sought therapy because she found it difficult "to cope with a male-dominated world." Although Joyce worked in a "female-dominated profession," social work, she felt the agency where she was employed as well as the national organization in social work to which she belonged helped facilitate the professional advancement of men but ignored women. As a result, Joyce found herself feeling alternately depressed or furious, resigned or rebellious. At the time treatment began, Joyce suffered from insomnia, anorexia, and phobias of the dark, heights, and animals.

In her treatment with me, Joyce initially formed a strong and positive transference. She felt that in contrast to her supervisors, colleagues, and family, I truly respected her. Feeling my support, she became more self-confident on the job and could accept herself as a woman with more equanimity. Liking her sexuality more, she began to derive more satisfaction from her relationships with men.

Following a six-month "honeymoon" in her therapy, and after referring to me constantly as a "mensch" (a decent guy), Joyce slowly began to compare me with her father, a rabbi, who "forced" his religious beliefs on her. She started to view me as one who "fostered a different religion, Orthodox Freudianism," and felt that psychotherapy was "a process of trading one piece of dogma for another." Although after a little more than a year of therapy her symptoms had disappeared, and despite her newfound gratification in her relationships with the opposite sex, Joyce became convinced I was *traif* (unkosher) and left treatment prematurely without resolving her negative feelings toward me and without understanding her Orthodox beliefs and practices.

As in all the cases I will be discussing, I will demonstrate how some of my negative countertransference reactions to Joyce supplemented the patient's feelings toward me.

Chapter 6 will summarize my findings and demonstrate that despite each patient's uniqueness, Orthodox Jewish patients share many similar dynamics. They all struggle with issues like compliance versus disobedience, idealization versus disparagement, cooperation versus competition, pleasure versus suffering, strong id wishes versus powerful superego admonitions. These conflicts are part and parcel of their Orthodoxy, but the Orthodoxy in many ways can serve as characterological armor that protects them against anxiety.

I will demonstrate in this concluding chapter how all the patients under discussion related to the therapist with the same ambivalence they unconsciously experienced toward their God. In most cases, by carefully analyzing their transference reactions, they could eventually enjoy their lives, including their religious lives.

In this final chapter I will try to demonstrate that if the therapist can approach religious behavior and religious fantasies in the same way that he or she views all behavior—dynamically, genetically, structurally, and topographically: that is, examines the patient's metapsychology—the Orthodox Jewish patient becomes a more loving and constructive human being who does not repudiate his or her religion but practices it more maturely and with more pleasure and flexibility.

A final conclusion will be that Judaism and psychodynamic psychotherapy agree on many issues. Both teach that self-enhancement and self-esteem can be obtained through self-awareness. Both agree that impulse control is necessary for mastery and maturity. Each has been in the position of a persecuted minority (Ostow 1982) and each refuses to be eradicated.

Just as Judaism has many divisions—Orthodox, Conservative, Reform, and Reconstructionist—so psychotherapy divides itself into many sects—orthodox Freudianism, neo-Freudianism, and many more. Perhaps as religion and psychotherapy learn to live with each other, they can begin to live with themselves in more harmony.

I am very grateful to many individuals who have helped make this book become a reality. First and foremost, I would like to thank my wife Marcia for sharing many ideas on Orthodox Judaism with me, and for editing and typing this book. Our sons, Professor Richard Strean and Professor William Strean, each made several constructive suggestions and criticisms. I would also like to thank Dr. Jason Aronson for his confidence in this project and express my appreciation to his editorial staff, particularly Norma Pomerantz and Judith Cohen for their splendid cooperation. Many colleagues, students, and supervisees gave me many valuable insights and shared many clinical experiences which were very informative. Finally, I would like to express my profound appreciation to the many Orthodox Jewish patients who have offered me rich opportunities to learn more about what it means to be a religious *Yid* or *Yidneh*.

1

A Psychodynamic View of Orthodox Judaism

Orthodox Judaism and Orthodox Jews have been the focus of attention of many scholars and writers. Philosophers have examined many dimensions of Orthodox Judaism's ideology (for example, Fromm 1950, Wolpe 1990). Sociologists and other social scientists have researched the social characteristics of Orthodox Jews (for example, Polsky 1960, Sklare 1960) and literary experts have written poignant descriptions of their emotional suffering, pathos, and passion (for example, Kahn 1968). Other experts from many other fields of endeavor have studied the religious ideals, practices, and contributions of "God's chosen people" and "the people of the book."

Although psychoanalysis and psychodynamic theory are close to 100 years old and despite the fact that its major, if not exclusive, interest is in people and their motives, conflicts, fantasies, ideals, and interpersonal relationships, the contribution to the psychology of Orthodox Judaism from psychoanalysis and psychodynamic theory is quite meager.

The first major contribution from psychoanalysis to an understanding of Orthodox Judaism came from Freud himself (1939) in his essay *Moses and Monotheism*. Here, Freud studied several characteristics of Orthodox Jews, particularly their "high opinion of themselves" and their "peculiar confidence in life" emanating from their "trust in God" (p. 105). Freud concluded that "it was the man Moses who imprinted this trait—significant for all time—upon the Jewish people. He raised their self-esteem by assuring them that they were God's chosen people, he enjoined them to holiness and pledged them to be apart from others" (p. 106). Freud alleged that it is to Moses that Jewish people owe "its tenacity of life but also much of the hostility it has experienced and still experiences" (p. 106).

In his study *Jokes and Their Relation to the Unconscious* (1905), Freud also was able to expose some of the fears, anxieties, superego pressures, and masochism of observant Jews.

A student and contemporary of Freud's, Theodor Reik, in several books (1931, 1941, 1951, 1959) focused on the unconscious fantasy life of Orthodox Jews. He showed that what was novel about the Jewish God was not that He reigned alone, but that He was perceived as the author and authority behind the collective superego that Moses created for the Jewish people (Ostow 1982). Reik also mentioned repeatedly that one of the major explanations for the strong attachment to God on the part of the Jews emanates from unresolved oedipal conflicts.

In his book *Psychoanalysis and Religion*, Erich Fromm (1950) made an attempt to integrate psychoanalysis and religion and urged the reader to try to find the issues that bind Judaism (and other religions) with psychoanalysis rather than to concentrate on their differences.

Two scholarly papers by Jacob Arlow (1951a,b), "The Consecration of the Prophet" and "A Psychoanalytic Study of a Religious Initiation Rite: Bar Mitzvah," furthered our understanding of the unconscious life of the observant Jew. In the first paper, Arlow revealed facets of the psychic life of those who became prophets of Israel. He considered also in this essay the nature of the relationship between the prophet and his followers, and the prophet's role in providing group ideals and common purpose. In his paper on the Bar Mitzvah, Arlow dealt with some of the sexual and superego problems that the Bar Mitzvah rite can induce.

Although there were a few articles from psychodynamic clinicians and theorists on Judaism during the next three decades, a major contribution from psychodynamic theory concerning observant Jews did not evolve until Mortimer Ostow (1982) edited *Judaism and Psychoanalysis*. In this comprehensive volume we have Arlow's previously mentioned two articles; a paper by Richard Rubenstein, "The Meaning of Anxiety in Rabbinic Judaism"; one by Martin Bergmann, "Moses and the Evolution of Freud's Jewish Identity"; and two papers by Ostow, "The Psychological Determinants of Jewish Identity," and "The Jewish Response to Crisis." Other contributions in this volume deal with monotheism, the similarities between Judaism and psychoanalysis, and the frequency of the hypomanic personality among Jews.

The most recent contribution from psychodynamic theory and practice on Orthodox Judaism is a book edited by David Meghnagi (1993) entitled *Freud and Judaism*. Again, the similarity between facets of Judaism and psychoanalysis is studied; there are papers on the psychodynamics of assimilation and anti-Semitism, and the Jew as an ethical figure; and pervading many of the papers is the notion of the powerful superego that is a prominent part of Orthodox Jewish psychic life.

One of the main reasons for the paucity of literature on Judaism in general and Orthodox Judaism in particular coming from the psychoanalytically oriented is that Freud and many of his associates vigorously rejected the Jewish religion (Ostow 1982). Although many analysts reject Judaism (and other religions) on scientific grounds Greenson (1992) and Ostow (1982) have contended that the majority of psychodynamic theorists and clinicians are Jewish, and in their search for self-esteem, they want to disavow their affiliation with Judaism. In effect Ostow has implied that many Jewish analysts and therapists are phobic about their Jewishness.

In contrast to the past, we are now living in an age when religion is being more accepted by the wider culture. This increasing tolerance affects therapists, who, like everybody else, internalize many of the values of what is currently in vogue. One of the most popular books of the 1990s was *The Culture of Disbelief* by Stephen L. Carter, who demonstrated how American law and politics have until recently trivialized religious devotion. Carter has argued for a just balance of mutually respectful forces, which should be a victory neither for religion nor for secularism.

Parallelling this perspective, current clinicians (for example, Bergmann 1982, Grossman 1993, Malony and Spilka 1991, Meghnani 1993, Ostow 1982, Smith and Handelman 1990) have been taking the position that religion in general and Orthodox Judaism in particular warrant the deep study and understanding that psychodynamic theory can provide. As psychodynamic

theory and practice and Orthodox Judaism have become
less estranged from each other, it behooves us to review
from a psychodynamic perspective some of the major
tenets and practices of Orthodox Judaism and determine
what can be useful to us as we conduct therapeutic work
with observant Orthodox Jews.

In our attempt to offer psychodynamic hypotheses
regarding the unconscious meaning of Orthodox Jews'
behavior, it should go without saying that a comprehensive study of all of the major characteristics of Orthodox
Judaism and Orthodox Jews would be an overambitious,
grandiose, and perhaps impossible undertaking. Rather, I
focus on and present my own interpretation of those
characteristics of Orthodoxy that consistently confront
clinicians, as culled from the literature as well as from
therapists who have treated Orthodox Jews. The reader
should recognize that this chapter is a modest one, designed essentially to present background information that
will make him or her a little more knowledgeable and
comfortable reading the next several chapters, which are
clinical studies focused on the dynamics and treatment of
Orthodox Jewish patients.

What Is Orthodox Judaism?

Although "Judaism" is difficult to define, most would
agree that it is a religion. But what is "religion"? Religion
has been variously defined as a faith, an identity, a hope,
and an overwhelming passion (Fromm 1950; Kahn 1968,
Wolpe 1990). Usually, if not always, a religion entails the
worship of a God. The God is supernatural in virtually
every religion, and is perceived as omnipotent, omni-

scient, and deserving of unambivalent obedience. Most religions require its adherents to pray to the supernatural deity (Greenson 1992).

Judaism certainly conforms to the aforementioned definitions of religion. Although Judaism has several denominations, Reform, Conservative, Reconstructionist, and Orthodox, the oldest of Jewish denominations is Orthodoxy. The term was first applied in 1807, when Napoleon was freeing Jews from the ghettos of Europe. It described Jews "who accepted the fullness of Jewish law and tradition" (Kahn 1968, p. 132).

Orthodox Jews view the Torah as divine revelation, a direct creation of God's hand. It is to be obeyed and believed without question. Orthodox Jews pray three to eight times a day and live a life replete with prayers, taboos, rites, rituals, and rules (Birnbaum 1964). The Orthodox are the most disciplined of the Jews and they stand for positive, old values. The men usually wear beards, yarmulkes (skullcaps), and all Orthodox Jews have a constant, deep, and private understanding with their God. They never question God's existence. Orthodox Jews support several hundred private Jewish elementary and high schools as well as several universities. Prayer, ritual, and strict regulations surround eating, sex, dancing, use of transportation, bathing—virtually every form of human activity imaginable. Men and women, girls and boys have strictly defined role-sets.

Having alluded to some facets of Orthodox Judaism, we still need to define Judaism. As Kahn has said: "Although Jews, or most Jewish leaders, argue that the question of a meaningful definition is significant and relevant in the United States today, [a] definition explodes beyond boundaries of time and place" (1968, p. 51).

One of the reasons that Judaism, here talking about

other than Orthodox Judaism, is very difficult to define is that it means many different things to many different people. Although one of the doctrinal foundations of Judaism is monotheism, there are many Jewish atheists. Despite the fact that many Jews consider affiliation with a synagogue a *sine qua non*, there are secular Jews who do not belong to synagogues, shun the rituals, yet feel a kinship to the Jewish group and its traditions. Biblical conceptions of God vary from book to book, and interpretations of Jewish law also vary a great deal. It has been said that there are gastronomic Jews who love Jewish food, cardiac Jews who have a Jewish heart, and Orthodox Jews.

For the Orthodox Jew, the subject of this book, practicing Judaism leaves time for little else—praying frequently, observing complex dietary laws, observing the Sabbath (which includes refraining from many mundane activities, such as traveling), and following many other taboos. Furthermore, "Orthodox Jews tend toward the arrogance of the devout. Their very devotion forbids the concession of error" (Kahn 1968, p. 135).

Major Characteristics of Orthodox Judaism

Belief in God

In a way that argument cannot alter, the belief in one God is central to Judaism. God is eternal and supernatural. Usually considered a male, He made the world. Each act of God, according to Jewish law, was and is for the benefit of human beings. However, humanity and God participate together inasmuch as God is dependent upon human beings for influence in this world. Divine reliance is an ancient teaching of Judaism, and God needs the efforts of humanity in His quest for the moral perfection of the world (Wolpe 1990).

In Numbers, a book of the Torah, that is, one of the five books of Moses (Genesis, Exodus, Leviticus, Numbers, and Deuteronomy), a passage reads, "When God was alone in the universe, He yearned for the company of His creations" (Numbers 13:6). In effect, the Bible tells us that God was a lonely parent who yearned for children. Orthodox Jews, and for that matter many other Jews, often refer to themselves as "Children of Israel." God, although King of the Universe, is also occupied with each individual person, like a devoted mother or father, concerned with each unique child.

The God of Jews is a jealous God and frequently commands, "You shall have no other gods before Me." The Orthodox Jew says the following prayer several times a day, "Hear O Israel, the Lord our God, the Lord is one." God wants to hear from his "children" and therefore requires constant praying. He always listens. Although arbitrary and unpredictable, He is never indifferent or deaf (Wolpe 1990).

In contrast to gods in other religions, the Jewish God is portrayed as a person with feelings. In Deuteronomy, He weeps while talking to Moses. In Genesis, God smiles broadly as he relaxes after having spent six days working hard creating the world. God's anger, jealousy, fickleness, severity, dependency, and desire to nurture constantly remind one of a very emotive and extremely dedicated parental figure who always is in desperate need of his children's attention and adulation.

The Jewish God is a rather narcissistic parental figure. Throughout the Bible we note that He is more especially the friend of those who care for Him. Rabbi David Wolpe (1990), in *The Healer of Shattered Hearts: A Jewish View of*

God, quotes a Chasidic leader, the Medzibozer Rebbe, who said, "As one thinks of God in his heart, so does God think of him" (p. 64). In Genesis, Abraham was called the friend of God because he dedicated himself completely to furthering God's interests in the world.

In Isaiah (65:1) God is described as fretting over the fate of his children as they are indifferent to Him: "I responded to those who did not ask, I was at hand to those who did not seek Me; I said, 'Here I am, here I am' to a nation that did not invoke my name." Wolpe (1990) suggests, "The quality of Divine concern includes all shades of relation; it takes on that peculiar worry and regard known only to parents" (p. 67).

The Orthodox Jew believes there is only one bond among individuals, the bond of being a child of God. Being God's children means that human beings are brothers and sisters (Birnbaum 1964).

Although God is the Father and King of the universe, He also created it. This "conceiving" the world, together with His constant tenderness, love, and care, seems to make Him a mother as well as a father. Stated Isaiah, "You shall be carried on shoulders and dandled upon knees. As a mother comforts her son, so will I comfort you" (Isaiah 66:12–13). The powerful attachment that Orthodox Jews have with God, communicating with the "Rock and Redeemer" constantly, is reminiscent of the strong symbiosis that a young child has with a mother. Just as the infant cannot let his or her mother out of sight, lest his or her world will be obliterated, Orthodox Jews cannot take leave of their God for too long lest their world will crumble. And, like the symbiotic parent, God loves those of his children who seek him out the most, those who, for example, pray to Him several times daily and compliantly obey His rules.

Similar to children who imitate and identify with their parents, Orthodox Jews imitate and identify with their God. It is written in Leviticus (19:12) "You shall be holy, for I the Lord your God am holy." Here, human beings are encouraged to be "godlike." In Judaism this usually means to be compassionate and loving. In a passage from Deuteronomy (11:22) the human being is exhorted "to walk in all His ways." And in Exodus (34:6) the traits of God that should be emulated are stated: "A God compassionate and gracious, slow to anger, abounding in kindness and faithfulness, extending kindness to the thousandth generation, forgiving iniquity, transgression, and sin." Several times in Deuteronomy the reader is implored to be as beneficent and as loving as God.

Despite God's omnipotence and omniscience, He does not arrange for the world to be perfect. Hence, Orthodox Jews, though devout, often practice their faith in anger. Like Job in the Bible who is "blameless and upright" (Job 1:1) but suffers many catastrophes, losing his children, his health, and his possessions, Orthodox Jews have forever been in an argument with God, furiously wondering why he has not been more beneficent. In the Bible, the prophet Habakkuk cries out, "How long, O Lord, shall I cry for help and thou wilt not hear? I complain to thee of wrongs and thou dost not help" (1:2–4). Wolpe (1990) states:

> The Jewish fury at God is not the vilification of an alien and hostile force. It is the distress and disappointment of being wounded by someone close. The Jews and God are locked in a lover's quarrel. Out of it is born the rich theme of protest and accusation against the One who represents ultimate justice. [p. 146]

Inasmuch as suffering endures and God seems to be silent on many occasions, the Orthodox Jew keeps trying harder, praying harder, and working harder to walk in the paths that the Almighty has directed. Then, God may become more kindly. Though infuriated at God for not granting permanent peace on earth and good will toward people, the Orthodox have a propensity to turn their venom against themselves and become even more devout, subservient to, and masochistic with their God. This is best observed in the preservation of the old tale of Abraham, who, to appease, placate, and ingratiate God, is ready to give up that which he most cherishes, his son Isaac. This planned sacrificial act denotes how the wish for God's love is so encompassing that the Orthodox Jew will give up almost anything to receive it.

Regardless of God's unresponsiveness at times, the expressions, "if it please God" and "with God's help" are used by Orthodox Jews in connection with all plans, hopes, promises, and wishes. Orthodox Jews who live constantly by faith and always feel the nearness of God make a habit of using these expressions no matter what they are wishing or deciding (Birnbaum 1964).

Because God is so much the ever-present parent in the Orthodox Jew's life, real parent–child relationships, though important, occupy less concern in the Bible and elsewhere than does the concern with God. The synagogue is often referred to as the "House of God" (Beth El), and many an Orthodox Jew can spend more time in God's home than in his own. In the musical *Fiddler on the Roof*, the leading character, Tevye, seems to spend so much time talking to God, thinking about Him, reading and learning more about Him, that he emerges as incapable of coping with many worldly matters.

God's Chosen People

At every Sabbath service and at many other occasions, Jews utter a prayer (*attah b'hartanu*) which means, "Thou hast chosen us." This prayer is based on many biblical passages that keep reminding the children of Israel that they have been chosen by God to be His witnesses, His kingdom of priests, a beacon of light and truth to the rest of the world. "You are a people holy to the Lord your God, who has chosen you from all the nations on the face of the earth to be his own possession" (Deuteronomy 14:2). Because they are God's "Chosen People," God has exclusive claim to Israel's service. In Chronicles 17:21, King David declares, "There is none like thee, O Lord, and there is no God beside thee . . . what other nation is like thy people?"

As already suggested, God's relationship with the children of Israel is reciprocal. For being "chosen," God's favor must be returned with complete devotion. Orthodox Jews, who acknowledge their dependency on God for all things, have a host of benedictions to meet every possible occasion. As Birnbaum (1964) states:

> There are scores of special benedictions to meet every possible occasion, from witnessing an electrical storm to seeing a great sage, Jew or non-Jew; from hearing good news to seeing the wonders of nature; from buying a new house to acquiring new clothes. Those who escape serious danger arising from illness or a perilous voyage recite a special benediction which reads, "Blessed are thou . . . who bestowest favors on the undeserving." [p. 105]

The Messiah

Originally, the term Messiah was applied to any person anointed to carry out the purposes of God such as a high priest or king (Leviticus 43). The title was given to the Persian King Cyrus, chosen to free Israel from the domi-

nation of Babylonia (Isaiah 45:1). Later King David of
Israel received God's promise that he would be the Messiah.

Jewish prayers are replete with allusions to messianic
hopes and aspirations. All prophets refer to the Messiah.
When the Messiah arrives there will be something close to
a utopia, a paradise regained. "No sound of weeping, no
voice of crying, shall ever be heard in it; no child shall die
there anymore in infancy, nor any old man who has not
lived out his years of life; he who dies youngest lives a
hundred years" (Isaiah 65:19–20).

The traditional outlook of Orthodox Judaism is that the
Messiah will provide an age of peace and plenty, and all
will blend into one brotherhood to perform righteousness
with a perfect heart (Birnbaum 1964). "On that day the
Lord shall be One and His name One" (Zechariah 14:9).

Despite many centuries of trying to understand God's
ways, Orthodox Jews acknowledge that they cannot fully
or even partially comprehend His motives or behavior.
This has been true since recorded time. As a passage in Job
(23:3) states: "Would that I knew how to reach God, how
to get to His dwelling place. . . . But if I go East–God is
not there; West–I still do not perceive Him."

From a psychodynamic point of view, the notion of a
God in Orthodox Judaism is a fantasy of those who
worship Him. The reason the concept of a God is an
imaginary notion is that He or She cannot be observed or
accounted for in any scientific sense. In psychoanalysis all
phenomena have causes and no one has been able to
demonstrate who God is and how God was created.
Therefore, to talk to someone or something that cannot be
reached by seeing, hearing, or with some other sense is
acting out an illusion (Freud 1927).

Inasmuch as living in this world always creates frustration, pain, disappointment, and oppression, we human beings have certain coping mechanisms to defend against anxiety and the realization that life is not consistently gratifying. One means of coping with painful reality is to imagine, to pretend, that is, to fantasy. A fantasy is a colorful embodiment of wishes, defenses, and superego injunctions. When children cannot tolerate being small, they fantasy they are Supermen and Wonderwomen. If they dislike their status as students, they "play school" and pretend they are teachers. Similarly, they play house, play doctor, and create those postures which reality does not permit them.

Just as a child who feels helpless in the absence of a mother or mother surrogate hallucinates a mother and then feels a diminution of tension, when a child cannot rely on his or her parents to provide the life circumstances he or she craves, an omnipotent and omniscient God is fantasied. From a psychodynamic point of view, the more helplessness, desperation, and fear we experience, the more we need someone to protect us. When reality offers limited consolation, we fantasy (Arlow 1979). The fact that so many individuals for so many centuries fantasy a God suggests that for ages, living in this world has been very difficult.

In the process of growing up, all children sooner or later realize their parents are limited people and not omnipotent and omniscient. To replace what they thought were godlike parents (Greenson 1992), children fantasize the image of God who becomes idealized, extolled, and imbued with all of the characteristics of a perfect parent. God, the new parent, can grant all the favors the parents did not or could not.

Inasmuch as Orthodox Jewish parents maintain that so much resides in the hands of God, rather than in their own interactions and transactions with their children, they encourage their children to turn the synagogue into a home and God into the powerful and idealized parent. Because God is a parental substitute, particularly for the Orthodox Jew, He has more of the human qualities than do gods of other religions. As we pointed out earlier, the Orthodox Jewish God laughs and cries, frets and smiles, and is an exacting taskmaster who rewards and punishes. He really serves in loco parentis—God, psychodynamically speaking, is a foster parent.

The more omnipotent we make God, the more impotent and helpless we become. If God is everything in our minds, we regard ourselves as next to nothing. Inasmuch as the Orthodox Jewish God influences and controls every facet of living, the Orthodox Jew feels extremely vulnerable without His or Her protection. Consequently, Orthodox Jews, like helpless children, must summon God many times a day in order to feel some safety and security.

Inasmuch as Orthodox Jews need their God to be constantly available, they have created a narcissistic God who needs the children of Israel as much as they need Him. Because Orthodox Jews, perhaps more than any other religious group, need God so desperately, they have also assigned themselves the role and status of "God's Chosen People." To maintain their position of favor, they are ready to serve God much like a slave serves a master.

The servile position in which Orthodox Jews place themselves in relation to God leads to a great deal of masochism. If God is so superior to them, they then feel very subordinate, much like clinging, dependent children. Consequently, Orthodox Jews have to work very hard to ingratiate themselves with and appease God as much as possible. Because many of their prayers and wishes are frequently ungratified, as we have seen in our earlier discussion, Orthodox Jews have an angry relationship with God. However, when children feel anger and hatred toward parents whom they desperately need, they turn their anger inward and feel like "bad children." Orthodox Jews, constantly angry at their God until the Messiah arrives, but feeling guilty for opposing their omnipotent parent, are constantly feeling sinful and seeking forgiveness.

Masochism and Gender Problems

When faithful Jews are required to be obedient to an all-powerful God, they begin to resent their weakened position. No human being consistently feels pleased to have a close, intimate relationship with another human being and always be in an inferior position. Just as children compete with their parents, teachers, and physicians, and play at being moms and dads, instructors, and doctors and nurses, they can also "play God." Like the child who not only identifies with parents but competes with them as well, Orthodox Jews compete with God. Some of the arrogance (Kahn 1968), confidence (Freud 1927), and dogmatism (Greenson 1992) of Orthodox Jews may be attributed to their latent but strong protest at being so beneath God as He enjoys dominion over them from Heaven. Thus they often fantasy themselves as omnipotent and omniscient, that is, godlike.

However, when the Orthodox Jewish man resents, competes with, and opposes God, he is in the same psychological position as the young boy who hostilely competes with his father. On one hand, the boy wants to vanquish father, but on the other hand he needs, fears, and is beholden to father. When the young boy finds himself in an oedipal position that is not tenable, he symbolically castrates himself and submits to father, much like he believes his mother submits to his father (Freud 1905b).

It would appear that the struggle that every boy has with his own father is heightened for the Orthodox Jewish boy as he struggles with his Father in Heaven. If the Orthodox Jew fights with God, he is bound to lose. Like the defeated oedipal boy, the Orthodox Jewish man takes a negative oedipal or latent homosexual position with God. More and more, the Orthodox Jewish boy and later the man begins to feel like a masochistic, demeaned girl or woman next to God—castrated, humble, submissive, but loving, abiding, and idealizing (Nunberg 1955).

Yet, the latent homosexual position among Orthodox Jews must be repudiated by them. The Torah has several admonitions opposing homosexuality. In Leviticus, homosexuality is considered a sin. Therefore, the Orthodox Jewish male, though constantly feeling effeminate beneath God, must build defenses to denounce, repress, and suppress his wishes to be a woman. One institutionalized ritual to help the Orthodox Jewish man with his plight is a morning prayer he offers to God seven days a week: "O God, thank you for not making me a woman."

Another more pervasive defense utilized by Orthodox Jewish men to cope with their feminine position next to God is a powerful sexual segregation movement. Observant Jewish women must sit apart from men in the synagogue, do not take an official part in the service, and a congregation in order to begin prayer must consist of a minyan—ten Jewish males above the age of 13, that is, women are excluded. Among the Orthodox (and only recently permitted among the Reform and Conservative) women are not allowed to be rabbis, cantors, or hold an office such as president of the congregation. Many of the prayers and rituals, such as laying tefillin (placing phylac-

teries on the head and arms), are for Orthodox Jewish men
only. One of the few unique privileges of the Orthodox
Jewish woman is to light the candles on the Sabbath and
on holidays and make a prayer over them.

Sexual intimacy has many restrictions imposed upon it.
Orthodox Jewish women are segregated from men and
may resent men, albeit unconsciously. Their male counterparts experience much castration anxiety. Sexual relations cannot take place several days before, during, and
after menstruation. Nudity is decried and the notion that
sex is essentially for childbearing is promoted (Ostow
1982). Dancing between Orthodox Jewish men and
women is forbidden in case the woman is menstruating.
Hence Orthodox Jewish men dance among themselves,
unconsciously promoting latent homosexual bonds. It
should be noted that in the many books on Orthodox
Jewish ideology and practice, there are no references in
the indexes to "sex" or "sexual relations."

As we shall see in the case studies in Chapters 2 to 5,
Orthodox Jewish women can often feel like second-class
citizens, angry at men for their subordinate position but
unable to do much about it. Their position psychologically
is similar to the Orthodox Jewish man's vis-à-vis God—
subordinate, demeaned, but angry. Consequently, Orthodox Jewish men and women, because of their demeaned positions, have to cope with many sadistic and
revengeful fantasies. The extensive ritualism in Orthodox
Judaism may offer some means of coping with these
fantasies.

Rituals

Rituals are integrated into virtually every aspect of daily
life among the faithful. From the moment they awaken in

the morning until they close their eyes at night, Orthodox Jews are engaged in a series of compulsory rituals (Reik 1931, Rosen 1960). We have already referred to some of these rituals, such as the frequency of prayer, the many benedictions offered for all occasions, and the prohibitions against sexual activity during certain times of the menstrual cycle.

Although one can offer hundreds of examples of compulsory rituals among the Orthodox, such as fasting on the Day of Atonement, leaning at the Seder table at Passover, not wearing shoes during shivah (the mourning period for the deceased), rituals surrounding cleanliness are the most numerous. Throughout the Bible is the exhortation "Cleanliness is next to Godliness." Numbers 31:22–23 says, "Whatever can stand fire, such as gold, silver, bronze, iron, tin and lead, you shall put into the fire . . . But whatever cannot stand fire you shall put in hot water." Consequently, the cleansing of utensils is a constant activity among the Orthodox.

The act of taking a ritual bath in a *mikveh* (gathering of water) is called *tevilah* (immersion). A woman during her menstrual period is viewed as unclean from the moment her menstrual flow begins. After the cessation of the menstrual flow, she counts seven days. At the end of seven days, she performs the *tevilah* by immersing herself in a *mikveh* that contains no less than 240 gallons.

There are three types of ritual washing, mentioned in biblical literature: (1) complete immersion (*tevilah*) in a natural water source prescribed for married women following their periods of menstruation or after childbirth; (2) washing the feet and hands, prescribed for the priests in the temple service at Jerusalem; and (3) washing of the hands (*netilath yadayin*) before sitting down to a meal, before prayer, upon rising from sleep, after defecating or urinating, and after being in proximity to a dead body. Orthodox Jews have always regarded bathing and physical cleanliness as important, because the human body reflects the image of God (Birnbaum 1964). In Ezekiel (36:25) it is stated, "I will pour clean water over you to cleanse you from all your uncleanliness and from all your idols."

In Genesis (23:13) there is a term, *am ha-oretz*, one that is used to this day. Literally it means "the people of the land," but it is used to describe those Jews who fail to observe the rules of cleanliness.

What does psychodynamic theory have to say about rituals? Rituals (Freud 1905, Ostow 1982, Reik 1931) are a regressive form of behavior to ward off thoughts, feelings, or actions that conflict with superego commands. It would appear that rituals among the Orthodox Jews are overdetermined. As we suggested earlier, the masochistic position required of Jewish men and women inevitably arouses oppositional wishes toward God and the many proscriptions and prescriptions of their religion. By having many rituals to perform under the eyes of their God, Orthodox Jews can deny their sadism. Like children who are frightened of their anger toward their parents and use the defense of reaction formation, saying, "I love my parents and their rules and regulations," Orthodox Jews deny their anger and proclaim their love for God through countless rituals. As Ostow (1982) states, "Ritual is a device employed when individuals fear a tendency to fail to perform a necessary act, or a tendency to perform a destructive act" (p. 168).

When one thinks from a psychodynamic perspective of the many rituals around cleanliness in Judaism, one can infer that the excessively clean person would really like to be dirty. If children are angry about rules and regulations being arbitrarily imposed on them, they regress to the anal phase of development and have fantasies of urinating and defecating on those around them—particularly on those who impose the rules and regulations in the first place. However, these urges conflict sharply with superego mandates, and the child, to cope with the intense anxiety aroused, becomes excessively clean. The Orthodox Jew, we can surmise, is excessively clean in order to defend against soiling or urinating in a sadistic fashion.

Rituals also can serve as a defense against separation anxiety. Children develop all kinds of rituals at bedtime or when going to school. They love to hear the same story read in exactly the same way night after night. Or they may concoct all kinds of ritualistic embraces with their parents before departing for school of for some other place away from home. Rituals for the Orthodox Jew, like rituals for the child, represent sameness and continuity and tend to ward off loss and/or change (Mahler 1968, Ostow 1982). Through rituals, the faithful Jew can maintain a symbiosis with God much as the child maintains a symbiosis with his or her parents.

Preoccupation with Orality

Oral activities are emotionally overdetermined in Judaism. The ancient Hebrews prescribed laws surrounding eating and to this day they remain one of the predominating disciplines of traditional Judaism. This preoccupation is without parallel in any other Western religion (Rubenstein 1982).

Some of the most enjoyable moments in Orthodox Jewish life are around oral activity such as the eating and drinking at the Passover feast (the Seder), at Sabbath meals, and on holidays like Purim, Hannukah, and Sukkoth. Yet, some of the most painful moments in traditional Jewish life involve oral deprivation. The faithful fast on *Yahrzeit* (the anniversary of a parent's death). Special importance has been attached to a fast resulting from "an evil dream." On the Day of Atonement, Jews fast as they ask God for forgiveness for their sins.

Many times while Orthodox Jews are enjoying themselves they have to stop and suffer some form of oral deprivation. At Passover, the enjoyable imbibing must be stopped by eating bitter herbs to remind Jews of the suffering of their brethren in Egypt. On their wedding day, an exciting day for most prospective brides and grooms, Orthodox Jews fast in order to repent for their past misdeeds (Birnbaum 1964).

Just as there is ambivalence about oral indulgence, there are mixed feelings about fasting. The Torah warns the reader several times that one must not fast excessively, lest the person become a public charge. It further points out that anyone who indulges in fasting is a sinner. A scholar may not fast except on the Day of Atonement for it interferes with study.

The story of Adam and Eve in the Garden of Eden serves as a paradigm to describe the emotionally overdetermined attitudes toward oral activity in Judaism. In Genesis (4:13) "eden" signifies delight and pleasantness. Because of its connection with the Tree of Life, the Garden of Eden has been regarded as the eternal home of bliss. It is filled with all of the delights of the senses, with streams of milk and honey, trees laden with all kinds of delicious fruits, and mountains bedecked with lilies.

Yet, the residents of the Garden of Eden, Adam and Eve, were soon banished for eating forbidden fruit. According to Genesis (5:22), God punished Adam and Eve for ingesting the fruit because they were too competitive with Him. Eating the fruit was symbolically acquiring knowledge and that made them come too close to being considered divine.

Food, like any valuable commodity, according to the Bible comes from God. Deuteronomy (8:10) states: "When you eat and are satisfied, you shall bless the Lord your God for the good land he has given you." However, as we learned in Genesis (5:22), the Lord seems to feel that consistent oral pleasure induces in consumers too much grandiosity, causing them such exultation and exhilaration that they begin to believe they are in heaven, like God!

As we have already suggested, there are numerous restrictions placed on observant Jews regarding eating. In Exodus (22:31) the Jew is told, "You shall not eat any flesh that is torn by beasts in the field." Three times the Torah declares, "You shall not boil a kid in its mother's milk" (Deuteronomy 14:21; Exodus 23:19, 34:26). This implies that milk and meat should not be eaten together. During Passover, the Jew is forbidden to eat leavened bread. (The evil impulse, *yetser ra*, is metaphorically called "leaven," which prevents men and women from doing the will of God.) When Jews remove all leaven from their homes, they are removing evil inclinations from their hearts (Proverbs 20:27).

A psychoanalytic view of the observant Jew's preoccupation with orality would first aver that because orality is the earliest stage of development, the Orthodox Jew's heavy concentration on oral matters may be interpreted as a powerful regression from more advanced states of psychological functioning. As we have pointed out, the phallic/oedipal competition with God activates tremendous anxiety and the faithful have to retreat from this anxiety. The regression to the anal period creates another anxiety and the defense is an overconcern with cleanliness. Although cleanliness placates the superego, it offers limited libidinal satisfaction to the person. Consequently, food and drink may provide the Orthodox Jew with some of the gratification that is missing from his or her sex life and other dimensions of living.

Although the God of rabbinic Judaism has been essentially a Father-God (King of the Universe), God is also a feeder and a nurturer. Therefore She is also a mother who sustains life. Inasmuch as Orthodox Jews are in a symbiosis with the Mother-God, like all oral babies they not only want to suck at her breasts, but also have wishes to eat her up (Klein 1957). As the Orthodox Jew's oral wishes intensify in his or her close and intimate relationship with a maternal God, he or she is prone to have many cannibalistic fantasies. When the Torah suggests that Adam and Eve will become too much like God if they eat the forbidden fruit, this seems to be a superego injuction against eating up God, the Mother. Like the child who says, "I love you so much I could eat you up," the Orthodox Jew is terrified of eating God up and worries about God's wrathful punishment, like the one imposed on Adam and Eve.

In "The Meaning of Anxiety in Rabbinic Judaism," Rubinstein (1982), speaking of oral cannibalism in Jewish life, says:

> The child's project is not merely to eat but to consume its environment [so] that the hideous pains of hunger which thrust it into reality will be appeased and sated. Its greatest unspoken fear, unrefined by experience or concept, is that this nourishing environment will do unto it as it has done. The cannibal child is in terror of a cannibal world, the world of the Mother. It is that

world which we see objectified in the religions of the Great Mother. Something of that world never disappears in later life in any of us. [p. 100]

Erich Neumann (1955), in his book *The Great Mother*, has suggested:

Just as the world, life, and soul have been experienced as a generative and nourishing, protective and warming Feminity, so their opposites are also perceived in the image of the Feminine, death and destruction, danger and distress, hunger and nakedness, appear as helplessness in the presence of the Dark and Terrible Mother. [p. 122]

In sum, a psychoanalytic interpretation of the centrality of oral preoccupations in traditional Judaism sees God not only as a Father in heaven but as a Mother, as well. Because life at higher levels of psychosexual development poses many conflicts for Orthodox Jews, they have a strong tendency to regress to orality. At the oral level with their symbiotic wishes to Mother God strong and with their cannibalistic fantasies activated, "the children" of Israel need many defenses to protect them against their temptation to eat up Mother God. Thus, they must repress and deny many of their oral wishes. This they do by fasting a great deal and by avoiding all kinds of foods and food mixtures. Yet, if and when Orthodox Jews suffer, Mother's chicken soup, like manna from heaven, "cures all ills from a sore throat to athlete's feet" (Kahn 1968, p. 25).

As Rubenstein (1982) states in one of his concluding remarks in "The Meaning of Anxiety in Rabbinic Judaism," "The mother is the first object of anxiety by any reading of psychoanalytic literature, religious history, or mythology" (p. 102).

The Jewish Superego

Permeating Orthodox Judaism—its writings, philosophy, and ethical principles—is a preoccupation with justice, righteousness, charity, and The Golden Rule. To read the Torah is in many ways to read about prescriptions for appropriate and proscriptions against inappropriate, interpersonal behavior.

Inasmuch as Jews have suffered much oppression throughout their history, such as at the hands of the Egyptians, Greco-Syrians, Romans, Nazis, and others, they feel highly indebted to their God who has saved and sustained them. Therefore, they owe the Lord the promise of leading a godlike life. Every Sabbath, Jews read from the Torah: "Remember that you were once a slave in the land of Egypt, and that the Lord your God brought you out from there by a mighty hand and an outstretched arm; therefore the Lord your God has commanded you to observe the Sabbath" (Deuteronomy 5:15).

The constant reference to the exodus in the Bible is explained by the fact that the redemption from slavery in Egypt was the greatest event in Jewish history. It marked the birth of the Jewish people and signified God's providence in Israel's struggle to stay alive (Birnbaum 1964). Psalm 137, which represents a memorial of the bitter experiences of exile, contains the well-known promise to God, "If I forget you, O Jerusalem, may my right hand be forgotten! May my tongue cleave to my palate if I remember you not, if I place not Jerusalem ahead of my joy."

Although Psalm 137 commands Jews not to forget

Jerusalem, the implication is they should not forget God and what He has done for them. Otherwise mutilation ("right hand be forgotten") and extreme oral deprivation ("my tongue cleave to my palate") will be the deserved punishments.

One of the main obligations of the Orthodox Jew is to be charitable. *Tzedakah* in Hebrew means charity and it is an historic duty of the religious Jew always to be charitable. The medieval Sephardic teacher Maimonides set down eight distinct degrees of charity. According to him, the highest order is the gift that assists the receiver to become independent. Then the scale descends—giving anonymously out of high motives, giving publicly to community charities, down to giving grudgingly, which is considered better than giving nothing at all (Kahn 1968). Stemming from *tzedakah*, philanthropy among Jews has become a gigantic establishment and social work is considered a particularly noble profession for Jewish men and women to enter.

Gratifying instinctual wishes just for libidinal pleasure is frowned upon among observant Jews. "Sacredness and not satisfaction is the end of life as traditionally conceived by Judaism" (Wolpe 1990, p. 19). Although holiness is an elusive goal, just out of reach, and is never achieved, Orthodox Jews tend to put happiness to the side and try, as best they can, to love God and worship His commands and commandments (Prager and Telushkin 1981).

Judaism very much endorses the idea of mutual aid. To be religious is to be community minded. A mitzvah, a good deed, is something the Orthodox Jew does daily— visits the sick, attends to those in mourning, aids the poor, and much more. Humility is considered the greatest of all virtues and the Messiah will not come until arrogance is obliterated. In the Jewish tradition human beings are godlike when they act with decency and compassion (Wolpe 1990).

Throughout the Bible are numerous statements and admonitions that one should treat people kindly, decently, and ethically. Hatred of any type is close to a sin, even when it is felt and certainly when it is acted upon. In Proverbs (14:31) it is pointed out that if anyone saves a human life, he or she is credited with having saved a whole world. An insult to a human being is an insult to God. The reader is further told that one good deed leads to another; one misdeed leads to another. "Do not despise any man."

Psalm 15 sets forth the character and conduct expected of the virtuous person. "The blameless man acts uprightly, and speaks the truth in his heart. He neither slanders nor hurts nor insults his fellow man. He has contempt for a rogue, and honors those who revere the Lord. He keeps his word at his own risk, and does not retract. He lends money without usury and accepts no bribe against the innocent. He who does these things shall never be disturbed."

The essence of moral perfection is best expressed by the prophet Micah (6:8), "What does the Lord ask of you? Only to do justice, to love mercy, and to walk humbly with your God." A corollary of Micah's admonition is the well-known passage from Leviticus (19:18): "You shall love your neighbor as yourself." In the same chapter the commandment of love is extended to the stranger. "You shall love him as yourself, for you were strangers in the land of Egypt" (Leviticus 19:34). In effect, the commandment of love applies to everybody and is the most comprehensive rule of moral conduct in Judaism.

The children of Israel were not permitted to hate even the Egyptians who had enslaved them. "Do not abhor the

Edomite, since he is your brother; do not abhor an Egyptian, since you were an alien in his country" (Deuteronomy 23:8).

The core of Judaism is the conviction that whatever is true is also good and beautiful. Telling the truth is frequently emphasized in the Book of Proverbs: "Truthful lips endure forever, but a lying tongue is only for a moment. A false tongue comes to grief . . ." (12:19, 17:20). In Exodus (23:7) the reader is exhorted, "You shall keep away from anything dishonest."

In the Book of Proverbs many forms of sinful behavior are enumerated: idle talk, offensive speech, evil thoughts, insincere confession, contempt for parents and teachers, fraud and falsehood, bribery, slander, arrogance, obstinancy, tale-bearing, groundless hatred, breach of trust. The confessions are phrased in the plural because the entire community regards itself as responsible for many offenses that could have been prevented. On the Day of Atonement, they are recited repeatedly to make the people intensely aware of the need for a fuller mastery over impulses. In Proverbs (28:13) it is written: "He who conceals his transgressions shall not prosper, but he who confesses and forsakes them shall obtain mercy."

Inasmuch as there is not a righteous man on earth who never sins (Ecclesiastes 7:20), a Jew is expected to make a confession on his deathbed. From birth to death observant Jews are forever trying to repent for their misdeeds.

Long before the advent of psychoanalysis, Jews seemed to have recognized something about internal conflict and the evolution of the superego. In Genesis (9:9), the good impulse (*yetser tov*) and the evil impulse (*yetser ra*) are discussed. They are pictured as wrestling in perpetual conflict within the human being. In talmudic literature *yetser ra*'s (or Satan's) function is to strengthen man's moral sense by leading him into temptation. In Genesis (2:7) it is mentioned that the existence of *yetser ra* in the heart of man and the struggle to overcome it lends high value to the good that emerges from the inner battle. The two conflicting impulses, the good and bad tendencies, are said to be implanted in man as a consequence of his having been formed from the dust and endowed with a soul.

In *The Ego and the Id*, Freud (1923) discusses how the superego becomes "an energetic reaction formation" against unacceptable id wishes. This appears to be very similar to how *yetser tov* tries to battle *yetser ra*. The superego according to Freud is the expression of the most powerful impulses experienced in the id. By this, Freud meant that the more punitive the superego, the more sinful and guilty the person feels, the more the person is fighting unacceptable id wishes—such as hateful and murderous desires and prohibited sexual wishes.

In his paper "On Narcissism," Freud (1914) referred to "the ego ideal," which measures the individual's actual ego. He pointed out here that what prompted the formation of the ego ideal was the influence of parental criticism, reinforced as time went on by those who trained and taught the child and by all the other persons of his environment who are "too numerous to reckon." The ego ideal is that part of the superego that affirms ethical imperatives; the conscience is that part of the superego that prohibits. The ego ideal says "Thou shalt"; the conscience says "Thou shalt not!"

In trying to appreciate the severity and intensity of the observant Jew's superego, the contributions of one of Freud's colleagues, Sandor Ferenczi, are helpful. Ferenczi (1955) felt that what was described by the terms "ideal," "ego ideal," and "superego" owed its origin to the deliberate suppression of instinctual urges that had to be denied and repudiated, while the moral precepts and feelings imposed by parental figures and others are paraded with exaggerated assiduity. Although this concept is painful to students of ethics and theologians, Ferenczi said that we could not avoid the conclusion that lying and morality are interconnected. To the child, according to Ferenczi, everything seems good that tastes good. The youngster has to learn to think and feel that a good many things that taste good are bad and to discover that the highest happiness and satisfaction lie in fulfilling precepts that involve difficult renunciations. Eventually all instinctual renunciation and all acceptance of unpleasure are associated with a feeling of untruth, that is, hypocrisy.

The primitiveness of the observant Jew's superego as would be explained by Freud and Ferenczi is because he or she has to repress and suppress many id wishes that are unacceptable to the ego. The emphasis on *tzedakah*, for example, can be viewed as a strong reaction formation against acquisitive impulses. It would seem logical that any human being who must obey many rules and regulations will want to rebel. *Tzedakah* and mitzvahs help the Orthodox Jew to repress and suppress selfish and egocentric desires.

In *Moses and Monotheism*, Freud (1939) concluded that the pervasive sense of guilt frequently seen in observant Jews could be accounted for as a reaction to murderous hostility toward the father. The sense of guilt, in turn, gave rise to "unusually stringent ethical ideals," which he saw as "characteristic . . . obsessional neurotic reaction-formations" (p. 134).

Ostow (1982) has taken the position that Jewish guilt can be further accounted for by the amount of tragedy that Jews have experienced. He states:

> Misfortune creates a feeling of guilt. This is a common
> clinical observation. The feeling of guilt seems to arise
> from a sense of helplessness and recedes when the
> helplessness recedes. It is this mechanism that ac-
> counts for the guilt frequently encountered in Jewish
> thought and writing. Where tragedy is absent in
> Jewish history, guilt does not appear. [p. 37]

Although Ostow's (1982) observation cannot be refuted,
it is incomplete. Freud (1921, 1930) has pointed out that
when tragedy is experienced, guilt-ridden individuals
blame themselves for it. Orthodox Jews, it would appear,
have punitive superegos to begin with. When they experience oppression and tragedy, which have been enormous in number and intensity, they blame themselves
and wonder, "Which sins are we being punished for
now?"

The concept that Israel suffers because of its sins can be
considered characteristically Jewish. Deuteronomy (23:1)
reasserts the principle of God's justice in the face of events
that might tend to question belief in it. If Jews suffer,
Deuteronomy avers, it is because they have sinned, not
because God is unjust.

In Judaism the doctrine of reward and punishment is
never challenged. When it seems inconsistent with reality,
then the Jew blames himself or herself for the misfortune.
Actually, Ostow (1982), in an essay, "The Jewish Response
to Crisis," suggests this himself.

> Clinical evidence demonstrates that guilt arises from
> the conflict between resentment against the protecting
> parent image who failed, and a wish, notwithstand-
> ing, to attempt to maintain a loving relation. In effect,
> [the guilty] and depressed individual says, "It isn't
> your fault, it's mine. Please take care of me." [p. 258]

What Ostow has stated above is pertinent to religious behavior. For theists, anger toward a loved and revered God is almost always repressed and then directed toward the self. Jews, particularly, because of their very strong attachment to their God, blame themselves for almost every disappointment; otherwise, they will feel in great jeopardy. Like children who prefer to feel intense guilt but keep their loving relationship with their parents intact and therefore will not aggress toward them, Orthodox Jews would rather maintain their punitive superegos, feel guilty much of the time, and not aggress toward their God who is their "Rock and Redeemer." As is suggested in Psalm 137, to which we referred earlier in this chapter, to show displeasure with God runs the risk of losing a hand and/or one's power of speech.

People of the Book

Judaism has a highly intellectual tradition where reason and rigorous thought have a central place (Wolpe 1990). Readiness to undergo all manner of privation in the pursuit of learning has always been a characteristic of Jewish students. As Birnbaum (1964) states: "Even a learned scholar must not think that he has reached his goal; he can always add to his knowledge. There is no pleasure greater than the study of the Torah" (pp. 367–368).

In Orthodox synagogues, serving the double function of study and prayer is the *bet ha-midrash* (house of learning), which is designed primarily for talmudic learning. In this house of learning, books are considered sacred, and nobody sits on a bench if there is a book on it. A book that falls to the ground is picked up and kissed. To put other things on top of a book is a sin (Birnbaum 1964). Books are associated with Almighty God and are cherished. To read and study is to be close to God.

Throughout the Bible, wisdom and a pure heart are linked. In Proverbs, Job, and Ecclesiastes are many statements which strongly suggest that character and learning are mutually dependent. The character of the scholar is supposed to rise above the level of the ordinary person, inasmuch as great thoughts spring from the heart.

To this day, Jews are proud to be people of the book.

> The greatest of American newspapers, *The New York Times*, has been a Jewish family property for [over ninety] years. Jews run perhaps half the major book publishing houses: Random House, Simon & Schuster, New American Library, Alfred Knopf, Atheneum are a few that thrive under the leadership of Jews. . . . From the astonishing three per cent [of the population], a quarter of the undergraduate student body at Harvard [is Jewish]. Practically all Jewish boys get at least some exposure to college. So many get advanced degrees that a Jewish dropout has been defined as an M.A. [Kahn 1968, p. 16]

Jews have tended to shy away from the physical, with few becoming professional athletes. But the verbal appeals to many; among lawyers, psychoanalysts, social scientists, and writers, for example, are a high percentage of Jews.

> Jews become teachers quite as naturally as Irishmen become corner cops, and usually for more noble reasons. In a tradition common to almost every Jewish community on earth, the teacher, the *melammed*, is accorded enormous respect. . . . Traditionally, the Jewish teacher embodies learning, symbolizes discipline and projects virtue. He is the inheritor and

> caretaker of knowledge, among people who revere
> knowledge next to the Almighty. [Kahn 1968, p. 92]

From a psychodynamic perspective, it is quite clear why Jews have remained the people of the book for many centuries. To read and study is to be loved by an omnipotent and omniscient God. Reading, researching, and studying, in the unconscious, is having a mutually loving, adoring, and rewarding conversation with a beloved parent. In many ways, study for the observant Jew is similar to a return to paradise, where knowledge becomes like sweet fruit and delicious milk. In effect, the Orthodox Jew while engaged in study is being fed by a nurturing and loving Mother/God and concomitantly praised for it by an approving Father/God. This appears to be a fulfillment of every child's dream—to be surrounded by two loving parents, both doting on the youngster with everybody in a state of bliss.

As the observant Jew studies, not only is he or she being loved by mother with father's approval but oral wishes are being gratified and the ego is on friendly terms with the superego. It is one of the few activities of the Orthodox Jew that is essentially conflict-free (Hartmann 1964).

Adding to the conflict-free learning activity of the faithful is the fact that ethical imperatives from the ego ideal are being obeyed. Observant Jews, in addition to the aforementioned gratifications, believe they are building their characters as they joyously study and feel nearer to their God. Their love affair with God makes them lovers of learning.

Success and Elitism

As Orthodox Jews acquire more and more knowledge, they assign themselves an elitist status that at times borders on arrogance (Kahn 1968, Wolpe 1990). Being chosen and part of an elite, Orthodox Jews have a self-confidence, a narcissism, that makes them value themselves and enjoy success of all types (Freud 1914, 1927).

As Kahn (1968) suggests, "Success surrounds and infuses their lives. Success in business, success in educating children, success in entering the most hotly-sought endeavors. Jews are business owners, business managers, professionals, writers and artists" (p. 15).

To some extent, the drive to succeed among Jews has an urgency and desperation. They pursue power, position, money, independence, and respect. To compensate for an underdog position, they aspire to power. Having been demeaned, detested, and oppressed for centuries, they want position. Having experienced much deprivation, emotional and material, they value money. Having been forced to submit to many tyrants, they want independence. Despite their obvious concern with success, the major preoccupation of Orthodox Jews is survival. To insure survival, they fight intermarriage, insist on the rituals being observed, and do everything they can to keep Judaism safe and alive.

The Orthodox Jew in Psychotherapy

Orthodox Judaism and psychodynamic psychotherapy have much in common. Both value the notion of continued self-assessment. The Talmud repeatedly advises that listening to counsel and receiving instruction are virtuous acts.

Those clinicians who have worked with Orthodox Jews in therapy note how eager the latter are to learn something more about themselves. Like Joseph in the Bible, they are interested in their dreams. Furthermore, they are usually convinced before embarking on a therapy course that knowledge will lead to a better life.

Although Orthodox Jews value the therapist as a guide and teacher, when they begin to idealize the therapist, many of them become worried about losing their faith in God and his commandments. As one patient asked his therapist, "Will I be converted from Orthodox Judaism to Orthodox Freudianism?" Another asked, "Is psychoanalysis a religion?"

One of the difficulties which Orthodox Jews do have in entering therapy is acknowledging that their religious modus vivendi has broken down somewhat. They can be uncomfortable with the notion that one rebbitzin commented on, "Maybe Orthodox Judaism does not have all the answers."

Orthodox Jews have been described as "people of terrible intensity" (Kahn 1968, p. 63). Though their outlook on life is unique and their responses to therapy different from the modal patient, they are also concerned with yesterday's parking ticket, today's headache, and tomorrow's television program. They have marital difficulties, parent–child conflicts, transference reactions, and resistances of all types—id, ego, and superego. As the pages that follow will demonstrate, Orthodox Jews are "more human than otherwise" (Sullivan 1953).

2

The Ambivalent Rabbi

It was a Monday morning in November when I received a phone call from a gentleman who introduced himself as Rabbi David Cohen. With a deep, resonant voice and serious demeanor, he said, "I'm familiar with some of your articles that appeared in the *Jewish Journal of Communal Service*. I'd like to meet with you." Not knowing the purpose of his call, I spontaneously asked, "Rabbi, do you want to discuss the articles?" There was a five-second silence and then the rabbi stated, "Well, maybe, but I . . . I . . . would like to meet with you to discuss some personal issues." Belatedly realizing that Rabbi Cohen was interested in a consultation with a view toward getting therapy for himself, I suggested, "Perhaps we can arrange an appointment to talk things over?"

In response to my invitation to meet at my office, Rabbi Cohen became quite hesitant. He told me he had a very busy schedule with meetings, seminars, consultations, and other ministerial responsibilities taking up much of his time. Sensing that the possibility of having a real face-to-face contact with a therapist activated quite a bit of anxiety in him, I tried to protect my prospective patient (Strean 1990) and asked, "Perhaps it would be easier to schedule an appointment at a time when your schedule is less crowded?" The rabbi replied, "You sound like an understanding man, Dr. Strean. Maybe I'll look over my schedule and get back to you."

As I reviewed my reactions to our phone conversation, I immediately got in touch with what was going to be a constant counterresistance problem (Strean 1993). Because David Cohen was a rabbi, I did not want to view him as a patient but more as an authority or senior colleague who would guide me! My first response on the phone about whether he wanted to discuss the articles demonstrated quite clearly my reluctance to become Rabbi Cohen's therapist.

I reminded myself that in the past, when I had received phone calls from other professionals such as accountants, professors, or physicians, I did not expect to have discussions with them on areas of mutual professional interest. Why did a rabbi's call induce a very different response? It did not take much work on my part to recognize that part of me did not want a rabbi for a patient because it seemed too much like a reversal of roles. "I want the rabbi to teach me, to support me, to help me," I confessed to myself. "He's the father confessor, not I." All of my experiences with rabbis, I concluded, were ones in which I transferred onto them parental qualities that at times were godlike. I joked to myself, "Sometimes you want to be a god, Strean, but you are not ready to treat God!"

As I reflected further on my phone conversation with the rabbi, I noted another countertransference response. Rabbi Cohen, to my surprise, was "more human than otherwise" (Sullivan 1953). Like all prospective patients, he was frightened to begin therapy. He had to impress me with his busy schedule, and his involvement in professional seminars and consultations similar to those in my life. "Rabbi Cohen wants to compete with me?" I said to myself in amazement. It was as if I were little Herby, feeling vulnerable, and that was the only role I felt comfortable in next to a rabbi.

Rabbi Cohen was the first rabbi who sought me out for therapy. I thought about him off and on for several days following the phone call. Most of my associations had to do with his not calling me back, and that if he did call I was not good enough for him. I had a host of other self-demeaning fantasies.

Like anybody else who berates himself, I knew that the aggression turned against myself had a defensive purpose (A. Freud 1946). The more I associated to my masochistic response, the more I could see that it served to protect me against feeling my grandiose fantasies. "Ha," I finally noted to myself, "if you can minister to a rabbi, you *are* feeling like God!" I realized that treating a rabbi was like treating my father or my father in heaven, God. "Quite a tall order," I told myself.

Rabbi Cohen waited a week before he called me again for an appointment. "I found a space in my schedule," he told me, and it turned out that I was free at the time he suggested.

Two days later, Rabbi Cohen arrived for his appointment, ten minutes late. He was slightly over six feet, with a dark suit, glasses, a yarmulke (skullcap), and a long beard. He looked older than his 40 years. Although his beard covered much of his face, he seemed to have pleasant features.

As he sat down, Rabbi Cohen apologized for being late and, shaking his head, commented, "I was counseling a married couple and the interview ran over. I guess you are used to that sort of thing." When I remained silent, the rabbi continued, looking away from me, "As I told you over the phone, I'm familiar with some of your writing, particularly the material on family relationships." Recognizing that Rabbi Cohen was relating to me more as a colleague than as a prospective patient, and wanting to make it safer for him to be with me, I asked, "Family relationships are an interest of yours?" He answered, "I could not fulfill my mission as a rabbi if I were insensitive to the strains and stresses on the contemporary family. By the way, I liked your comments on role incongruity between the sexes in your paper." After another silence, he said, "I'm not here exclusively for intellectual reasons. I have problems of my own."

On my showing interest, Rabbi Cohen told me that he found it difficult to "accept my wife Ruth the way she deserves." He went on to say that although Ruth was a pleasant person, a loyal wife, and a hard worker, she had "serious limitations." Then, looking at me somewhat apologetically, Rabbi Cohen became silent. After about thirty seconds of silence I asked him, "Is it difficult to talk about Ruth's limitations?" Rabbi Cohen, feeling somewhat reassured that I was not going to rebuke him for his resentments toward his wife, went on with his marital complaints. Reflected Rabbi Cohen, "Although I'm acutely aware of the fact that the sexual dimension of marriage is an important component of a positive relationship, it is lacking in our marital subsystem." After a few seconds of silence, he went on, "We participate in erotic interplay not more than once a month and, to add insult to injury, we have limited emotional interchanges. Pleasure is lacking."

When I asked the rabbi how long there had been limited pleasure in his marriage, he told me about his marital history as well as salient features of his personal life. Ruth and David had been married for fifteen years. They met at a synagogue where David was an assistant rabbi and Ruth was a congregant. Describing Ruth, David remarked, "She was nice looking, came from an Orthodox Jewish home, her father was active in the Jewish community, and her two brothers were observant Jews. (I noticed that David did not mention Ruth's mother, at all.)

Describing his marriage in more detail, Rabbi Cohen told me that almost from the beginning of their relationship, Ruth offered little gratification in bed, in conversation, or really anywhere. They had one son and hoped to have more children but "God had other plans." He thought their son Joseph would bring them closer together but this did not occur. At the time I met Rabbi Cohen, "Joe" was 7 years old. "Joe and I are not too close either. I think he reflects the lack of joy in our home. We all go through the motions of praying, observing the Sabbath and holidays, eating, working, studying, but we are not having fun," commented the rabbi in a depressed tone.

Rabbi Cohen's father was also a rabbi. "He was strict, rigid, and a disciplinarian. My mother, my younger sister, and I all catered to him," said Rabbi Cohen wistfully. Without making any connection, he described the atmosphere in his parents' home as extremely similar to his current home. Then, with his head down and on the verge of tears, David Cohen said, "I have something to tell you that I have not told a soul. I'm not too happy being a rabbi. Although my congregation seems satisfied with me, the

routine of enacting a very defined role, at times, seems
like drudgery. I've wondered if I would be better off being
a psychotherapist or something similar."

It was at this point that the time allotted for our
appointment was up. I told Rabbi Cohen I sensed that
there was a lot on his mind that he had not talked very
much about to anyone, and he heartily agreed. I then
asked him how often he'd like to get together with me. "I
think I'd only have time for one meeting per week," he
responded. He agreed to the fee I was charging and we
made an appointment without difficulty for the following
week. However, after we got up from our chairs, Rabbi
Cohen lingered. He went on to tell me some more about
his crowded schedule and emphasized how much counseling and teaching he did. I sensed once again that Rabbi
Cohen was feeling uncomfortable in the role of patient
and therefore he resumed a professional demeanor. With
this in mind, I commented, "You are a very active professional. Perhaps we can talk about that some more." Rabbi
Cohen then shook my hand, said "My pleasure," and left.

When Rabbi Cohen was delaying leaving my office, I
thought of a joke that helped me get in touch with some of
my countertransference difficulties (Strean 1993a,b). The
joke was, "One of the big differences between Christians
and Jews is that Christians leave and don't say goodbye;
Jews say goodbye but don't leave." Reflecting on the joke,
I realized that I was uncomfortable with Rabbi Cohen's
prolonging the session and that I even had some wishes
that he'd be a Christian and leave without saying
goodbye.

I started to examine how I related more to my patient's
defense of intellectualization, and his inability to take
responsibility for any of his marital problems, rather than
how he was yearning for love; and he didn't face this

sadness either but was trying to impress me with his busy professional schedule. Rabbi Cohen's controlled exterior was hiding a young, sad David, who did not know how to get love and was frightened of receiving it. I told myself, "This guy is very depressed and has been depressed most of his life. He's never faced this painful fact and no one has ever helped him face it. He comes from a cold, unhappy home and has participated in making his current home a miserable abode. He's far from my stereotyped rabbi who has it all together."

As will be recalled, even after my initial phone call with the rabbi, I became aware of much resistance to having him as a patient. Further reflection made me recognize that I was suffering from the outmoded notion that psychotherapy for a member of the clergy was sacrilegious. To probe the unconscious of a rabbi was not only being grandiose, like treating God, the Father in heaven, but it was entering into forbidden territory—like viewing the primal scene or some other place that I did not belong. Nonetheless, the challenge seemed great and I could empathize with the troubled soul that David seemed to be.

After the first session, to me Rabbi Cohen became David and sometimes little David. Rather early in our relationship I began to view him more as a boy and a son, and much less as a big man and father.

Early Sessions and Early Resistance

David came to his weekly sessions with eagerness and always on time. He had a lot to say and for the first six sessions I said almost nothing. He talked about his resentment toward his wife, who he felt had "little to offer."

"She seems like a little girl in one of my Hebrew school classes and I feel more like a father to her than a husband," David said with mild contempt. As David continued to make derogatory remarks about Ruth, it occurred to me that behind his chronic marital complaints were unconscious fears and wishes. I hypothesized that he needed his wife to be a daughter because a woman and wife would frighten him, making him feel like a little boy (Strean 1985a). I knew it was too early in the treatment even to attempt to work on this with him.

As I listened to David during his early sessions, I realized that my "dynamic inactivity" (Fine 1982), that is, my quiet listening, was helpful to him. No one in David's present or past gave him a full ear. Instead he had to listen to others and resented it. Unaware of his resentment, he became depressed. Talking to me without being forced to listen to my ideas lifted his depression and self-esteem because he felt appreciated in a way that was important to him.

Around the eighth session of our weekly meetings, David brought in his first dream. David recalled, "I was giving a sermon in the shul [synagogue] on Abraham and his wife Sarah and pointing out how we are all Abrahams and Sarahs. As I looked out at the congregation, everybody was listening attentively except for one man, sitting in the back, who was asleep." When I remained quiet (asleep), David began to associate to the dream. He knew that talking about Abraham and Sarah and their marital relationship had something to do with his therapy "because that is what we have been focusing on—marriage and marital conflict." As David had shown earlier, in addition to getting help for his marriage, he also wanted to be an authority on marriage, which he was making himself in the dream. I said to him, "When you are an

authority on marriage, which you appear to be in the
dream, most people are impressed, but there's one guy
who is going to sleep on you. What about him?"

David responded to my question by saying, "Next to
you, I'm no authority on marriage. I can impress most
people, but if you were in my congregation, you would
not be impressed." I responded, "Perhaps you worry that
you'd put me to sleep?" David's face reddened, then he
laughed, and then he said, "or maybe I don't even want
you to listen to me."

I thought David's interpretation was "right on!" He
wanted to do all the talking and shut me up because he
was afraid to hear from me. Inasmuch as he seemed quite
ready to work on the dream, I asked, "Are you a bit
worried about what I'll say to you?"

David reflected on my question and told me that next to
me he felt "like a junior." With some help he could share
with me that he felt intimidated by me, as he did with his
father. Rabbi Cohen Senior was "a very intimidating man
whose word was law." David went on, "He made me
study the Torah all the time, told me I must work hard for
God, and become a perfect Jew. If I ever made a mistake
he clopped me in the *ponim* [slapped my face]. Although I
revered him, I could never satisfy him. I could never talk
to him. I never did anything but honor my father and
mother. I had to observe all of the other commandments."

Although David was visibly relieved after discharging
much of his resentment toward father, he looked at me as
if waiting for a response. When I asked him what he was
feeling at the moment, he said, "I think I'm worried about
you criticizing me for my anger." I smiled and said, "No
wonder in your dream you want me to sleep. If I talk, I'll
criticize you."

David responded positively to my attempt to be a

benign superego for him and brought out more resentment toward his father, contempt toward his mother for never standing up to his father, and envy of his sister who did not have to cope with the many pressures that were imposed on him.

After his fifteenth session, David arranged to come for sessions twice a week. He felt less depressed and said that "our exchanges give me hope."

The Honeymoon Phase

For the next three months of treatment, David seemed to be a new man. In contrast to his depressed, obsessive demeanor, he was full of smiles, talked about enjoying his wife much more, and spending more time with his son Joseph than ever before. In addition, he found his pastoral duties to be less onerous.

As has often been noted (Fine 1982, Strean 1985), when a patient in psychotherapy feels given to and understood, he or she wants to give to and understand others. David was feeling like an appreciated and loved son and therefore could be more of a father to Joe. As his own vulnerabilities were tolerated and not condemned, he could relate with more kindness to Ruth. And as he felt compassion from a professional, he became a more humane professional with his congregants. Several times during this phase of treatment he talked about the pleasure he derived from singing with the choir in the shul, dancing at the weddings where he officiated, enjoying the food of the Sabbath meal, and "finding God smiling in His Heaven."

During the seventh month of therapy, David had a

profound insight that was of enormous help to me in my
further work with him and has been a valuable tool in my
work with all religious patients. Commented David, "My
picture of God varies. When I'm in a good mood, He is in
a good mood. When I'm angry or depressed, He does not
seem very kind. When I feel pressured by all of my
rabbinic duties, He actually looks malevolent."

David's transference to God shifted during his therapy
as his therapeutic transference shifted. Many times the
transferences were similar; sometimes they split (Kernberg 1976), whereby God was the loving parental figure
and I was the hated object, or vice versa. Rabbi David
Cohen helped me really understand that a human being's
view of God is an expression of his or her own self-image
and self-esteem.

As David felt more loving toward his family and congregants, they became more loving toward him. This in
turn further reinforced David's self-worth, and the spiral-
ling effect was obvious to him and those around him.
Toward the end of David's eighth month of treatment, he
commented heartily, "I'm really loving my neighbor and
myself"—a slight modification of a biblical injunction.

When David started to come to treatment twice a week,
he immediately felt a sense of optimism. His dreams,
almost all with Jewish content, reflected his shift of mood.
In one dream, he was lifting a heavy Torah and demon-
strating his virility. In another one, an attractive woman
was admiring his tallith (prayer shawl), and in one dream
where he was giving another sermon, I was smiling
approvingly.

On examining his dreams, David saw how he was
feeling "virile and phallic." In this connection, he brought
out how very small and weak he felt next to his hypercrit-
ical father and unsupportive mother. He recalled several

childhood memories, all of which had him trying to please God, parents, and teachers with little love forthcoming and much criticism always a possibility. As he voiced his resentment and began to realize that I was interested in understanding him rather than in judging him, the past with its misery seemed to contrast with the present's growing pleasures.

What was happening to David Cohen was, of course, not unique. Reuben Fine (1982) introduced the notion of the "honeymoon" phase of treatment to describe what most experienced clinicians have observed. When a patient has been the recipient of attentive, empathetic listening, he or she feels a sense of optimism, has many insights, and discovers dimensions of his or her psyche that until now had been repressed. There are several reasons for the evolution of this positive state of mind.

First, unlike most relationships in which patients have been involved, in the therapeutic encounter all the attention is on them. When they are with their therapists, patients do not have to be concerned with other people's dilemmas, conflicts, and exhortations. This kind of relationship induces in most patients a feeling of importance and offers some narcissistic satisfaction. Second, when patients unburden themselves and discuss embarrassing moments, shameful episodes, and infantile fantasies, the sensitive therapist does not judge or criticize them; he or she listens and tries to understand. When guilt-ridden, self-effacing individuals who expect retribution, condemnation, and attack for their real or imagined transgressions receive in session after session warmth, kindness, and empathy instead, they begin to feel liberated (Fine 1982, Strean 1990).

As I thought about David's "honeymoon," I realized that although the honeymoon phase is ubiquitous, it had more meaning for him. His Orthodox Jewish background, which helped strengthen his very punitive superego, made him always ready to be put down and punished. Psychoanalytic therapy prescribes just the opposite—a nonjudgmental attitude, understanding, and no punishment. Therefore, he felt enormously lifted.

David, like most honeymooners, wanted to see his partner as much as possible. By the ninth month of treatment, he was seeing me three times a week and was on the couch. He was in full-fledged psychoanalytic treatment.

On the Couch

Although David initially welcomed lying on the couch and free associating, and despite the fact that looking further at his dreams and fantasies provided him with new insights, by the beginning of his first year's anniversary in therapy, the honeymoon was over. David began coming late for sessions, there were long silences in many of them, and from a warm enabler I became, as he experienced me, "a pompous ass."

When David's strong resistance to the analysis was apparent to both of us, I suggested to him that he was probably having feelings toward me that were difficult to express. This was around the fourteenth month of treatment and David had expressed discouragement about everything—his work seemed arduous again, his wife and son irritated him, and as much as he thought his therapy could help him, he was now quite pessimistic about it. However, my suggestion that he was holding back feelings about me seemed to help him.

"I really resent lying down here, feeling so small while you can sit there and take it easy while I squirm," commented David. "I get the feeling that you think you are some giant while I'm some dwarf. What an unfair, unequal relationship this is!" he said.

In one of his dreams, David was trying to restrain a young boy from using a slingshot and hurling a rock at a teacher in his Hebrew school. Associations led to his own past when he would have liked to throw rocks at his own teachers and perhaps do the same thing to his father. I brought the dream into the transference and asked, "Do I seem like a Goliath to you, David? Would you like to sling me?" After a laugh, David said, "Yeah, I'd like to be King David instead of little David and I'd like to knock you out. You take up too much room!"

At this stage of treatment, although David was resenting me intensely, I was feeling warmly toward him. He induced in me the feeling I often had toward both of my sons when they were teenagers and feeling their oats. They were strong and confident enough to take on the old man. Just as I knew I had provided some safety and security for them to be able to openly compete with and defy me, I felt the same kind of pleasure in my work with David.

Interspersed with David's hostile explosions at me were more memories of father's sadistic attitude toward him and his sister, Mary. "He had no real understanding of kids," lamented David, "and neither did my mother. She was more his slave than a wife."

In one of David's dreams during the sixteenth month of treatment, he was saying the Kaddish (the prayer for the dead); however, the room where he was praying was unfamiliar and "the place was definitely not a synagogue." Although it took some time (a couple of sessions) for

David to identify where he was reciting the Kaddish, eventually he could tell me that the building was on 89th Street. When I reminded David that (at that time) that was the street where the New York Center for Psychoanalytic Training was located, the analytic facility with which I am affiliated, David asked himself out loud, "So what am I doing saying Kaddish in a psychoanalytic institute?"

David's further associations to what we both frequently referred to later as "the Kaddish dream" enabled me to interpret to him that he wanted to turn my psychoanalytic institute into a synagogue, take it over, and say Kaddish for me. David confirmed my interpretation by saying, "I guess I come here not to praise you but to bury you!" Although David did not continue his recitation of Shakespeare's oration—"the evil that men do lives after them"— he did feel many pangs of guilt for wanting to kill me. Ruefully David commented, "I feel very morose about the idea of your dying. I think a lot of people would miss you. Furthermore, I feel like a Haman (an anti-Semite who was a prime minister of a biblical king, Ahasuerus, and who eventually met his downfall) and I suppose . . . you know . . . 'An eye for an eye, a tooth for a tooth.' " David clearly saw himself as a killer and was sure I would seek revenge. Further, he appeared to feel very omnipotent and grandiose about his murderous wishes. It was as if his thoughts not only could kill me, but they already had because he was feeling morose and reciting the prayer for the dead! His affect was depressed because in his mind he had already committed a sin (Brenner 1955).

In my work with David and in subsequent therapeutic contacts with Orthodox Jews, I learned that very often "the word is the deed." Although it certainly is not unique to Orthodox Jews to distort the meaning of thoughts and wishes and think of them as deeds—it is a derivative of the magical thinking of children in which we all participate occasionally—it is stronger in Orthodox Jews. As I listened carefully to David and tried to understand his strong conviction that he really did kill me, and that was why he was depressed, I eventually could understand what was going on in his inner life. Because David's murderous wishes toward me, the Goliath of his fantasies and the punitive father of his memories, were so strong, he *wanted* to believe he had killed me. For David, who felt very oppressed by all kinds of giants, his rage was intense and pervasive. He wanted to murder so much that he derived some hidden gratification from believing he had already done so (Strean and Freeman 1991).

By the middle of David's second year of treatment, he was beginning to see that he wasn't as powerful as he thought. Just because he wanted me dead (as he wanted his hated father, Haman, Goliath, and Hitler dead—all of whom I represented at one time or another) did not mean that he had magically pulled the trigger and gotten the desired result. In one subsequent session, after he came close to believing I was going to live for awhile, I could say, "Rumors of my death are somewhat exaggerated."

The several months of treatment that we have just reviewed could be viewed as the first treatment crisis (Fine 1982, Glover 1955). The first treatment crisis is characterized by a negative transference and is caused by many factors. Just as lovers after a honeymoon are required to accept the hard fact that their partners cannot gratify all of their wishes, many patients become furious with their therapists who have not supplied them with sufficient relief, reassurance, and rewards. In addition, just as some lovers cannot tolerate the pleasures of being loved and given to consistently and have to provoke arguments to relieve themselves of guilt, there are some patients who cannot tolerate their therapists' nonjudgmental, caring attitudes and seek to provoke the therapists into punishing them. Further, just as children are shocked when adults do not reprimand them for their fantasies, many patients are shocked that their therapists, who are often experienced as parental figures, do not reprimand them for what seem to them to be real sins (Strean 1990).

It would appear that all of the aforementioned issues were operative in David's first treatment crisis. On the couch he felt less given to than hitherto in therapy; also he felt very vulnerable and on the spot. He was sure he had hurt me, maybe killed me, and wanted punishment, and finally, it was hard for him to accept that there was a superego around that was less punitive than his.

As David eventually felt like less of a killer, it ushered in a new phase of treatment.

The Latent Homosexual Transference

Having aggressed toward me for a fairly prolonged period and having not received the anticipated punishment, David's transference became increasingly positive. He talked again of feeling particularly close to his son Joseph and implied that he could feel this way with Joe because he was now experiencing me as a benign father. In one of his dreams in which he was hugging his son, he mentioned that it was his way of telling me he wanted to be my Joseph. Here he was referring to the biblical Joseph who was his father's favorite and was envied by all of his brothers. "I want to be your psychoanalytic Joseph and I want all of your patients to envy me," said David with some agitated enthusiasm.

When I waited for more associations from David regarding his wish to be my favorite son, he began to ingratiate himself with me as he did in his childhood with his father. First, he had dreams in which he arranged for me to receive awards in his synagogue for being a humanitarian and an outstanding professional. Then he started to refer patients to me from his congregation. Analysis of the dreams and wishes to refer me patients suggested a deep yearning for a father's love and approval that at times seemed close to desperate.

On my sharing with David my impression that his strong wish to have me be his loving father had undertones of anguish and despair, he began to weep. In between sobs, he told me how much he always wanted his father's love, but it was hardly ever there. "My father could never hug me, kiss me, compliment me, or support me. After awhile I gave up on him and began to feel that God was my loving Father. Sometimes I fantasy God hugging me, but it fades away. I want something and somebody real."

By the time David's analysis was well into its third year, he was having many homosexual fantasies and dreams. Sometimes he was a little boy sucking at my penis and saying, "Your juices make me strong." On other occasions, we were having anal intercourse with "your stiff *putz* up my *tochis*." From time to time David expressed the wish to be his sister or mother with me "because being a boy or a man is too much work."

It took much courage for David to face the girl in himself, and it was with much anxiety that he told me about his homosexual fantasies. Frequently he projected his punitive superego onto me and had me critical of him for his desires. He mentioned repeatedly that the Bible did not look with much favor on homosexuality and he reported how in his morning prayers, like all devout Jews, he thanked God for not making him a woman. David commented wryly, "I thank God every morning for not making me a woman and I come to my psychoanalyst and tell him that I wish I were a woman. Something's wrong." I told David I thought he was genuine about both issues. He wanted to be a woman and didn't want to be a woman. Responded David, "I guess I'm the case of an ambivalent rabbi," and mildly chuckled.

I had recognized in prior clinical work as well as from my personal analysis that when competition with the father is very intense and the hostility toward him is great, the father was insufficiently emotionally available during the boy's formative years. If a father is emotionally available, the son doesn't want to kill him with as much fury as David showed. David's homosexual longings were strong, I could infer, because he had missed out on consistent and loving fathering.

I very much empathized with David's hunger for a father, and he could feel my understanding. Also, as he felt less frightened of my judging him negatively for his wishes, he could be more open about his fantasies. This was very liberating for him because he had used much energy in trying to defend against his passive homosexual wishes.

When David feared the girl, woman, and little boy in himself much less, he could relax more with his wife Ruth and they began to have more frequent sex. At first David referred to his more enjoyable sex life as a mitzvah (a good deed). Sex became less of a superego mandate later in treatment when he referred to sex as *shepping nachas* (having pleasure).

"What Kind of a Jew Are You?"

As is true of most patients who are members of minority groups and wonder just how genuinely accepted they are by the therapist, Orthodox Jews are very curious about how Jewish is the therapist. David was no exception.

By the latter part of his third year of treatment, David, who assumed I was Jewish, asked me, "What kind of a Jew are you, anyway?" Being well socialized to the norms of psychotherapy, he knew I wouldn't answer him, so he began to associate to his own question. "I suppose you are an infidel like Freud and all your mentors," David hypothesized. "I sometimes think you married a shiksa (a gentile woman) and that you are bringing up your children as heathens. I bet your home is not kosher, I don't think you are affiliated with a synagogue, and maybe you are not even circumcised," David further conjectured.

As David fantasied about my Jewish background, there was a thinly veiled contempt in his demeanor. In many ways he was mocking me for being an unobservant Jew. When he associated further to my not being circumcised, I was able to interpret to him that he seemed to want to circumcise me so that, in effect, he would be castrating me.

David acknowledged that he was angry at me for not being an Orthodox Jew (although he had no concrete way of knowing what the facts were). "We have less in common, and that bothers me. We cannot be brothers under the skin. We cannot be warm friends, colleagues, or a symbolic father–son dyad," he cried out. He suggested, "You are an ambivalent Jew. You don't know if you are coming or going. I think most therapists are very confused about religion."

Although I did not question the accuracy of David's assertions about my ambivalence or my colleagues' confusion, I felt quite certain that David was projecting some of his own ambivalence onto me and others. Inasmuch as projection is a very primitive defense, it rarely can be interpreted at first blush. Usually it is important, if the treatment is going to be preserved, to let the patient project onto the therapist, with the therapist remaining as nondefensive as possible. When the patient sees that the therapist can subject himself or herself to examination without too much defensiveness, the patient eventually does so (A. Freud 1946, Strean 1990).

I asked David if he had any thoughts about how I became so ambivalent about Judaism. "Sure I do," he said quite confidently. "You probably had an authoritarian father who induced a lot of mixed feelings in you, so you became ambivalent about God and religion. You also had a nice Jewish mother who cooked good chicken soup, so you haven't revolted because you have a taste for Jewish stuff. You have been too influenced by Freud and his gang, who were too scientific and didn't have enough heart."

David had further hypotheses to offer about my limitations as a Jew. He suggested, "You, like most people in this day and age, are quite hedonistic, and Orthodoxy does not particularly endorse 'the pleasure principle,' 'libidinal gratification,' and other id pleasures. Maybe your ego is not strong enough to cope with frustration."

As I remained quietly reflective, David slowly began to consider his analysis of me. He began to wonder about how much we did have in common, after all. Perhaps psychoanalysis was making him question his own views on Orthodoxy.

David's Doubts about Judaism

Toward the end of David's third year of treatment, he began to seriously question how much he wanted to continue being a rabbi, whether he truly believed in God, and about the wisdom of observing the Jewish rituals.

It was after David acknowledged that possibly both he and I struggled with ambivalence toward Judaism that he had a dream that contained this theme. In the dream, David brought a Bible to an analytic session and started to rip the pages out of it in anger. As he looked at my face in the dream, he could not tell whether I was condoning or condemning his ripping the Bible apart, and he felt quite confused.

Analysis of David's dream suggested that he had always had some reservations about several of the tenets of religious dogma. Furthermore, the dream suggested that he was angry about submitting to the edicts of the Torah. He began to wonder where God had been during his life. "If God is so good," David asked, "why hasn't He been kinder to me? He seems like my absent father and ineffectual mother. He wants so much from me and all his children—prayer, devotion, rituals—and what does He give back? Just like the old man and the old lady!"

In another dream, instead of saying a prayer on washing his hands, he urinated on the floor, suggesting that he wanted to rebel like a defiant child who was being severely toilet trained. Regressing further, David had a dream of eating a bacon and tomato sandwich on the Day of Atonement, thus refusing to fast and not eating kosher food, both at the same time.

For periods during this phase of treatment, he quit praying and told me several times, "God and I are not on good terms these days. We are not talking to each other."

When we were analyzing his rift with God, David also mentioned that many times during his teenage years he had fantasies of not speaking to his parents. He never carried out these plans, but he was using his current rift with God to displace some of the anger he felt toward his parents for being unrewarding and ungratifying.

Although I did not realize it at first, David was experiencing me as an ally in his battle with God and Judaism. In one of his dreams as he was yelling at his congregants for being too dogmatic in their beliefs, he had me applauding him. When I asked why he thought he arranged in his dream for me to support his fight with God and Judaism, David was shocked. "I thought you'd be pleased to have me fight with God and religion, and now you question what I'm doing?" David asked indignantly.

Not feeling my support in his war, David felt both furious and helpless. "Now I have nobody. No God, no parents, no therapist. I'm on my own!" Although David was feeling very agitated, he was moving toward increased autonomy and an identity shaped by his own values—not imposed on him. Nonetheless, he was very upset with me for being neutral in his religious war.

The Reappearance of the Negative Transference

David always seemed to need an enemy. When he stopped fighting with God and Judaism, he fought with me and psychoanalysis. He did not seem able to get along with Judaism and psychoanalysis at the same time. As he began once more to attack psychoanalytic theory and treatment, and psychoanalysts, I suggested to him that he always seemed to need a parental figure to battle. Without realizing it, David confirmed my interpretation by saying, "You don't know what you are talking about. I'm for the truth and you are for some 'ism.' "

As David continued to demean me, it became clearer that underneath his anger was a sense of futility that there was no omnipotent, omniscient, consistently loving and lovable parent available to him. On having a dream in which his son Joseph was looking in a department store to find a Santa Claus who would gratify him and love him, David and I both became clear that Joseph was a stand-in for David himself. He wanted a loving parent but could not find the parent in Judaism or psychoanalysis. So he went outside the synagogue and outside my office to find that parent. Seeing what he was ready to do to find a loving parent, David joked by asking, "Is this a conversion symptom?"

Although David had spent most of his treatment discussing his father and experiencing me much of the time as a father in the transference, he began to talk more about his mother. Now in the fourth year of treatment, in one of his fantasies David gave me breasts. Associating to this fantasy, he told me that although his mother was "not a strong, assertive, or emotive woman," she "made good food." Despite his not having any conscious recollections of breast feeding, David thought his mother was "a good nurturer."

As David began to relive memories of his mother, it became clear that although he experienced her as a good nurturer, he did not believe she was emotionally available enough. "She seemed just to want to cook, clean, and feed us. We could not talk to her," David said ruefully. He did not feel that his sister Mary was closer to his mother than he was, and he knew from conversations with Mary that "a lot was missing for her, too."

As David reflected more about his mother's coldness, in the transference he wanted me to be the mother he never had. He had wishes that I rub his back, stroke his hair, and tell him how much I cared for him. Although these wishes aroused a great deal of anxiety in him, as was true of David throughout the treatment, he "hung in there" and worked on the issues. In his dreams at this time he made me into famous women therapists such as Melanie Klein, Anna Freud, and Frieda Fromm-Reichman. On my asking David about these analysts and what they meant to him, at first he joked and said, "They are all Jewish." I said, "Maybe you'd like me to be a Yiddisheh Momma?" thinking of the lullabye by that name. At this, David wept and talked about his deep yearning for "a warm, kind mother, who could also talk to me."

David had memories of his mother as one who was very concerned with toilet and bodily functions. He reported, "Whenever anything went wrong, she would say, *'Gay pish'* [Go urinate]. She also inspected our bowel movements. The other thing she did that made me uncomfortable was that she walked around in her underwear. Sometimes she would ask me to fasten or unfasten her bra. I even got the feeling when I was about twelve that she wouldn't have minded if I gave her a *shtup"* (had sex with her).

As David reminisced about his mother, it became clear that although she was not too emotive, she was seductive. When David could reexperience his mother's seductiveness in his treatment, we were able to see why he had avoided Ruth sexually—he had made Ruth a mother and sex with her in many ways felt like incest.

Working Through and Termination

After David spent some time working on the maternal transference, expressing repressed emotions of both a

sexual and an aggressive nature, he returned to a recon-
sideration of his relationship with his father. Instead of
feeling so much anger toward his father, he began to see
him more as he was—an "unhappy, insecure man who
had his strengths, too." Eventually, he could take a similar
stance about his mother. "Not a bad *Yiddisheh madel*
[Jewish girl], a little scared, a little dull, but a little sexy"
was his assessment. He always respected his sister Mary
but did not have much to say about her.

As David's marriage and relationship with his son
Joseph were now much more enjoyable, as his self-esteem
had improved, and as his work as a rabbi became consistently more meaningful to him, David and I agreed that
after five years of treatment, we could terminate our work.

Although David's religious views as well as his religious
behavior were essentially the same as when he began
treatment, his transference to God had changed and his
feelings about rituals and prayer had greatly modified. He
thought about God much less but "felt His quiet presence." He was no longer in any big battle with his parents
or with me. Rituals, prayer, and religious observances
became times "to have fun with people, to communicate,
and to love."

David spent several months reacting to his terminating
treatment. He "hated leaving" much of the time, but felt
"it was necessary to grow up." He knew that I had always
enjoyed working with him, and both of us were pleased
with his results from treatment.

I have heard from David on three occasions since he left
treatment. As he said on the the phone the last time I
spoke with him, "I'm enjoying working and loving."

3

The
Masochistic
Rebbitzin

I entered the waiting room of my office suite and saw a petite woman in a black dress with her hands wrapped tightly over her face. When she heard my footsteps, she quickly released her hands and look startled. She smiled anxiously and in a voice hardly audible, asked meekly, "Are you the doctor?" I responded, "I'm Dr. Strean." I then asked, "Are you Mrs. Abramowitz?" She nodded her head and I could now see a young lady with a pretty face and dark hair, and a woman who looked like a terrified little girl.

Mrs. Rachel Abramowitz, after being invited into my office, walked slowly on her tiptoes as if she did not want to disturb anyone. On my showing her the chair where she would sit, she sat down very carefully as if, once again, she did not want to disrupt something.

After a silence of about twenty seconds, I asked Mrs.

Abramowitz if she could tell me what prompted her to seek me out. She explained that her family physician suggested that she receive psychotherapy "because my body doesn't work well." I wondered out loud what was going on with her body and she told me that "off and on" for the past eight years her heart had beat so rapidly that often she was convinced she was about to have a heart attack. Sometimes she thought she was going to faint because she was so "breathless and helpless." In addition, during the same period of eight years, Mrs. Abramowitz had recurrent bouts of diarrhea, constipation, and nausea. As she told me of her symptoms, Mrs. Abramowitz began to blush profusely and to stammer, as well. Although I did not comment on her blushing or stammering, she said, stammering, "What's happening right now happens to me a lot when I'm with people. The words do not come out and my face gets very red."

Although Mrs. Abramowitz was quite forthright about her symptoms, I wasn't sure how she felt about being referred to a therapist. I asked, "Was it your physician who wanted you to come to see me?" After answering in the affirmative, Mrs. Abramowitz told me that the physician had informed her there was nothing organic about her bodily dysfunctions and he decided she was "tense" and "needed to talk to somebody." I asked her how she felt about the physician's recommendation and Mrs. Abramowitz replied without affect, "All right."

Although our interview had begun only about ten minutes ago, I already had a strong impression of how my prospective patient conducted her life. She seemed very compliant but not too aware of what she was feeling beneath her polite exterior. I said to myself, "Her heart problems and stomach disorders are probably her way of expressing intense emotions that she can't put into words."

I returned to Mrs. Abramowitz's earlier "All right" in response to my question about how she felt about her physician's recommendation. I commented, "Sometimes a recommendation to get therapy can be difficult to accept." Mrs. Abramowitz, with a serious expression on her face, responded, "I always do what I'm told." I asked, "Whether you like it or not?" "Yes," she answered, "that's the best way to get along." I said to myself, "Even if it causes you bodily aches and pains!"

I tried to stay with Mrs. Abramowitz's excessive compliance as it was being expressed in the "here and now" of our interview. I stated, "You have to come and see me whether you like it or not. Perhaps you can tell me how it feels being here," trying to help her verbalize her tremendous anxiety, which was obvious from the moment she walked into my waiting room.

Mrs. Abramowitz told me she had never been in psychotherapy, but her physician told her she would have an opportunity to talk about herself. She then told me that she had never talked about herself with anybody before. She came from a family of eight children and "there wasn't time for any of us to really talk too much because someone else would always interrupt." Her father, a cantor, "was usually rehearsing, praying, or working with the choir, so he didn't talk to us very much." Her mother was very busy "cooking, cleaning, sewing, and praying" and therefore she did not have much time for her children either. Rachel was the fourth youngest, with two younger brothers, one younger sister, two older sisters, and two older brothers. She was "not close to any of them."

Rachel attended a Hebrew parochial school and then

went on to Yeshiva University where she majored in Jewish history. She told me she was an average student. However, when I explored this further, I discovered she had superior grades, B's and A's. She considered herself average because she did not contribute very much to the class discussions.

After graduation from Yeshiva University, Rachel worked in a private high school where Hebrew was spoken almost all the time. She taught Jewish history and thought it "was nice." She dated a lot while in college and later, too. All of "the boys" were "nice." She married Nathan, who was a rabbi, when she was 27, and at the time that she began treatment had three daughters, aged 7, 5, and 3.

I realized that the beginning of Rachel's somatic symptoms eight years ago coincided with the time she got married. I asked her, "How have these last eight years been, with a husband and three young children?" Rachel replied that she tried to be "a good rebbitzin," went to the synagogue frequently, and that she always knew "my place." I told Rachel that I wasn't sure I knew what "your place" was. Rachel blushed and with a very slight note of sarcasm in her voice said, "The place of a rabbi's wife is to smile nicely, sit quietly, pray hard, and be a loyal servant of God." When I remained quiet, Rachel looked at me and said, "You are probably thinking that isn't very much fun!" I asked, "Is it?" Again Rachel blushed and said, "It's all right."

Everything seemed "all right" or "nice" with Rachel, even though it was fairly clear that she was repressing and suppressing many intense feelings. Even when it was toward the end of the session and I asked her how she had experienced her interview with me, inasmuch as being with a therapist was something new and different for her, she answered, "All right." On my asking her how often she wanted to come and see me, she told me that the physician had suggested twice a week. I knew for now that if I asked her how she felt about the recommended frequency she would have said "All right." So I said instead, "I have the impression that you like to follow orders, particularly from a doctor. Perhaps we can try twice a week and see how that works out for you." In what was her characteristic response, Rachel said "All right" and agreed to pay the fee I requested.

In contrast to my usual response to a first interview with a prospective patient, which is one of enthusiasm, when Rachel left my office I had a headache. As I subjected my symptom to examination, I had several associations. My first was the realization that in some way I was identifying with Rachel. She had arranged to give herself psychosomatic symptoms and I was doing the same thing. Why? When I thought of why I would turn myself into a Rachel, a memory that haunted me throughout my childhood and adolescence emerged. I remembered getting a dollar bill every Passover from my grandmother while my close cousin Joan got only fifty cents. It was a screen memory for the guilt I often experienced as a Jewish boy who had it better than my cousin and other Jewish girls who were my contemporaries. Boys had privileges and pleasures in and out of the synagogue that girls did not have, frequently were held in higher esteem by family and others, and while I enjoyed the superior position, it gratified too many of my competitive and aggressive fantasies.

Rachel's meekness, compliance, inhibitions, and nonassertiveness aroused my guilt. I was better off than she was, I reasoned, and was enjoying this fact too much. Rather than acknowledging some of my sadism, I became masochistic like Rachel. But my masochistic defense helped me get in touch with what I was sure was Rachel's rage toward her husband and father, who did not seem to relate to her with very much concern or warmth. I could appreciate how every Orthodox Jewish woman, particularly a rabbi's wife, had to defer to the man, and resented it. As I studied some of my countertransference reactions further, I realized that what I did not want to allow into consciousness was the part of me that felt like Rachel's husband Nathan, a man who sounded authoritarian and seemed to have contempt toward women.

One of the hypotheses I had about Rachel's somatic symptoms was that they masked her rage. In many ways she probably resented being a rebbitzin but could not admit this to herself nor to anyone else. Perhaps when she enacted the role of rebbitzin her blushing defended against her sadistic fantasies, which she did not want to reveal. Maybe, I thought, she wanted to tell people off but couldn't—hence her stammering. When I reflected on her gastrointestinal difficulties, I wondered what she couldn't stomach and whom she wanted to shit on.

As I contemplated working with Rachel, I knew that it wouldn't be easy for her to relate to me. I had to be patient. However, I didn't know how right I was about this until the treatment got started.

"I Can't Talk!"

For the first three months of Rachel's twice-a-week therapy, she had enormous difficulty talking to me. There were long silences that made both of us uncomfortable, and a few times we both wondered if she could continue being in treatment, it seemed so painful. Each time she tried to talk to me she blushed, stammered, or became tongue-tied and silent.

When I attempted to help Rachel face her anxiety in the therapeutic situation by telling her that there was something similar in talking to me and talking to the congregants in the synagogue—both situations made her uncomfortable—she nodded but produced no material. If I suggested that being with me aroused anger in her, but it was very difficult to express it, she nodded but, once more, she could not elaborate.

After about a month of strong resistance on Rachel's part and dwindling patience on mine, it occurred to me that any effort on my part to get Rachel to talk was experienced by her as something akin to a rape. She did not want to respond to me no matter what I said or asked. I tested my impression by making a statement to Rachel without expecting a response. I said, "You feel under a great deal of pressure here to produce for me and it's a real struggle." To this Rachel smiled and relaxed in her chair. I followed this up with, "I think all of your life you have felt a lot has been expected of you and you are supposed to satisfy everyone around you." To this Rachel began to talk with a little bit of affect and averred, "My whole life I've had to follow orders and I've been scared that I wouldn't do things right. I'm always afraid that I'm going to be criticized."

I suggested to Rachel that one of the difficulties for her about being in therapy with me is that she felt I expected a lot from her and that if she didn't give it to me, I'd give her a hard time. Rachel commented, "I agree. I really cannot be myself with anyone. I always have to do what is required of me." Then, paraphrasing the Torah, she said, "What does the Lord require of thee. Do what everybody asks, walk and talk quietly, be kind, and never disagree!"

I responded, "The Lord wants a lot from you!" And Rachel said, "I'm His humble servant."

By observing Rachel's resistance to talking and what it signified (A. Freud 1946), and by studying my own counterresistances (Strean 1993), I was able to come up with a plan in which I could involve Rachel in treatment in a way that was now more palatable for her. She had resented talking to me because it meant producing for a demanding, unloving, and unlovable parent. In response, I was feeling like an impatient parent who was irritated at her for her nonresponsiveness. For this excessively compliant and frightened young woman, I had to become much more permissive and much less demanding. As I obeyed my own prescription and indirectly asked Rachel to obey nothing and not give me anything, our relationship modified. She stammered much less, her blushing disappeared, and she reported by the fourth month of therapy that her gastrointestinal problems had subsided appreciably.

Rachel's Prolonged Honeymoon

When Rachel became convinced that I was not going to force her to produce for me, she became much more trusting, and by the end of the fifth month of treatment, a positive transference was in full bloom.

The first dream that Rachel reported was that she was in a choir in the synagogue, singing with pleasure, and the choirmaster, one Herschel Stern, was nodding approvingly at her. Staying with my prescription to ask nothing of her, I waited to see what she would do with the dream. "My father, you know, is a cantor, so I guess I'm singing with my father," Rachel said reflectively. She then recalled the play *I Never Sang for My Father* and realized that in her dream she was gratifying a wish to be with her father within a friendly family—something that did not occur in reality. Rachel also told me that the choir her father supervised did not have any girls in it. I said, "In the dream you are feeling that you can be an equal to boys and sing for father." Rachel, for the first time since she had been in treatment, uttered words of anger. "All my life I have felt boys and men have all the good deals. They *daven* [pray] and God listens to them. I'm not sure He listens to women as much. We sit on the side in shul and I think we're like French fried potatoes while the men are steak."

After Rachel's anger had subsided, I mentioned that the choirmaster had a specific name, Herschel Stern. At first she though of Isaac Stern, the musician, and then went blank and blushed. I suggested that thinking about the choirmaster made her feel uncomfortable. Then Rachel laughed and said, "He had gray hair and glasses like you!" I then laughed and said, "And you gave him my initials— so I guess you've made me the choirmaster."

Rachel then shared with me that coming for therapy made her begin to think she was "a real person," that our conversations made her feel that somebody was really listening to her, and her mood was "much better."

Rachel spent the better part of the next six months "enjoying" her treatment. She spent most of the time venting anger about the emotional void in her family, how she never received much attention, and that she always had to be "a workhorse." She realized she had never questioned the demands made on her and had concluded by the time she was 8 or 9 years old "that all Jewish girls are refined maids who serve everybody but get very little in return." Very occasionally she made mild complaints about her husband Nathan, who was "hardly ever home, just like my father." As soon as she got in touch with some anger toward Nathan, she would defend him and point out that he was a very devoted and dedicated rabbi, serving God and his congregants "in an admirable manner."

In another dream Rachel had during this period, she was carrying a Torah in a procession of men. When she mentioned that carrying a Torah was "another one of those male privileges that women don't have," I reminded her that this Torah dream was similar to the one in which she was in a choir—she was involving herself in activities exclusively for Jewish males. Rachel then asked me, "Do I have penis envy?" I suggested, "Maybe you have Torah envy," keeping in mind that the Torah could be viewed as phallic in shape. Rachel then confessed that she often thought during her childhood that being a boy would offer her a better life.

She told me that not only did she want to carry a Torah and be in the choir, but she also wanted "to *daven* with the guys and pee standing up."

Rachel, toward the end of her first year of treatment, was becoming quite spunky. She was more accepting of her aggression, much less masochistic, had more self-respect, and had a good working alliance with me. I noted, however, that she had not talked much about her husband and had made almost no mention of her sex life with him nor of her sexual fantasies.

Rachel Faces Her Marriage

As we began the second year of treatment, Rachel, in response to my suggestion, increased the frequency of her sessions to three times a week and also decided to use the couch. She very much welcomed being on the couch, feeling that many of her long-held fantasies were being gratified. First, she was getting permission to relax, something that was rarely encouraged by anyone in her life, "present or past." Second, while relaxing she had "the full attention of someone who cares," another void in her life. Third, Rachel saw herself as "a member of the elite." To be on the couch, in analysis, meant to to her that she had many ego strengths. By now she was reading psychoanalytic texts and articles and had discovered that those in analysis had "the capacity to introspect, form a therapeutic alliance, and tolerate regression." Lying on the couch and free-associating was experienced by Rachel "as a gift from the good Lord." She had the fantasy that God in His wisdom had instructed me to suggest to Rachel to be on the couch in psychoanalysis.

After Rachel had been on the couch about two months, she had her first erotic transference dream. In it she and I were hugging and kissing, and although we both knew it was antitherapeutic and antireligious, we were "doing it anyhow." Rather than discussing her fantasies toward me, Rachel spent considerable time tearfully and angrily talking about how rarely she was hugged or kissed "in the past or present." ("In the past or present" was becoming one of Rachel's favorite phrases, clearly suggesting that to her, her past and present were not too different.)

Rachel told me that neither of her parents was particularly demonstrative and rarely did her siblings embrace each other. "Nathan is the same way," she complained. "He rarely hugs or kisses me and only gives the girls a peck once in a while. We hardly ever make love. Either he's reading or he's tired."

As I listened to Rachel complain about the lack of love

and sex in her marriage, at first I found myself feeling angry at Nathan as if he were the villain and Rachel was the victim. I had several fantasies of rescuing Rachel from her marital woes. Most of the time, in my fantasies I would show her how an attentive and loving husband would act. Inasmuch as Rachel was young enough to be my daughter, I also had competitive fantasies toward her father as well. I'd be her good father and good husband—not too far away, I recognized, from being an omnipotent God.

As I studied my countertransference fantasies further, I realized that although I might get some childish gratification in joining with Rachel against the men in her life, nothing would have been more damaging to her than if this were acted out. She needed to become aware of why she married a man who colluded with her to have an essentially sexless and loveless marriage.

I reminded myself again that behind every chronic marital complaint is an unconscious wish (Strean 1985). "What has made it safe for Rachel to have the kind of marriage she does?" I asked myself several times. As I was pondering this question, Rachel provided me with an answer through a dream she had in the sixteenth month of therapy. In the dream, Rachel and I were once again kissing and hugging and then we abruptly stopped. On my asking her why she thought she arranged for us to stop pleasuring each other in the dream, she answered, "I don't like taking any initiative, particularly in lovemaking. I want the man to do that. Do you remember when we first started with this therapy, I couldn't talk? You had to take the initiative. Although I did not tell you at the time, what was going on with us reminded me of sex with Nathan and me. It hardly existed. He doesn't do anything about it and I don't either."

As I reflected on Rachel's anxiety and inhibition about taking initiative, I thought first of Erik Erikson's (1950) conceptualization of a developmental task that he called "initiative versus guilt." I wondered what Rachel would feel guilty about if she took some initiative sexually or elsewhere in her life. My next thought was, "She seems afraid of her aggression; throughout her life she's been a very masochistic servant. If she takes initiative, she'll be giving up her servile status and that will feel very frightening to her." I essentially trusted my hypothesis but had no definitive proof of its validity.

In his *Interpretation of Dreams*, Freud (1900) pointed out that dreams are the "royal road to the unconscious." Rachel proved Freud correct in many of her dreams, including one in her nineteenth month of treatment. In the dream Rachel was sitting in the women's section of the synagogue but was getting restless listening to a sermon being delivered by Nathan. "Rather than just sit there," she climbed over the pew, walked onto the *bimah* (the altar), and jumped on her husband. As she attacked Nathan, the elders of the synagogue, all men, pulled her off. While being pulled off, she saw me standing by, "rather impassively," and she said to me derisively, "See what happens when I take initiative!"

Rachel and I spent several sessions working on the dream. It helped us understand much better many of her sexual inhibitions, difficulties in asserting herself, and conflicts in her marriage. Later in treatment, on several occasions, each of us referred to this very important dream, which was a royal road to many of her unconscious wishes, defenses, and superego admonitions.

To take initiative was extremely dangerous for Rachel. It was crossing many forbidden boundaries. She would be defying one of the rules of Orthodox Judaism if she "did not stay in her place" and continue to sit in the women's section. Not only did taking initiative make Rachel feel that she was a defiant sacrilegious woman, but she would also experience herself as a violent man because in the dream she went to the men's section of the synagogue. Further, to take sexual initiative with Nathan was the equivalent of raping him, and that certainly seemed forbidden, as well.

Rachel's dream also revealed that if she relinquished her masochistic status she would be defeated by many men. They would team up against her. Although the dream showed that Rachel felt bored by her husband's moaning and groaning, and wanted to do something about it, she felt angry at me for encouraging her to take action. "See what happens when I take initiative," she said sarcastically, as if to put me in my place.

When Rachel and I worked further on the dream, I called her attention to the fact that just as we discovered early in the treatment that she felt pressured by me to perform, in the dream she was taking initiative primarily to please me and was angry at that. It was not too different from being placed in an unacceptable position in the synagogue.

Rachel began to see that she was relating to Nathan, me, and the rest of the world as if, in many ways, she was a little girl and everybody around her was either a big parent or God Himself. Consequently, she had to submit to everybody else's wishes and commands. This induced much anger, and whenever she thought of taking some initiative she felt like a slave breaking out of her master's strict controls. She would then feel close to violent and this scared her very much.

Able to accept her destructive wishes with less anxiety, Rachel became more able to assert herself and to enjoy her normal, healthy aggression. She began to take more initiative with Nathan both sexually and interpersonally. Although he did not have too much resistance accepting her suggestions to go to the movies, to watch a TV program together, or to discuss their daughters' problems, he became virtually impotent when Rachel started to demonstrate that she was interested in sex with him.

When Rachel saw that Nathan wanted to avoid sex completely and not discuss it with her, with much courage she persisted in trying to make Nathan face his own contribution to their essentially celibate life. At first he attacked Rachel and criticized her for being badly influenced by a Freudian sexual maniac, that is, her therapist. However, Rachel was able to find quotes from articles and books of learned rabbis implying that "sex in marriage is a mitzvah." Nathan then tried to believe his problem was physical, but a physician showed him otherwise. Finally, he went for psychotherapy himself and faced his own sexual and emotional conflicts.

Although Rachel and Nathan began to have a much better marital relationship by the time Rachel had completed two years of treatment, a latent and problematical issue in her marriage and elsewhere became the focus of her treatment.

In a session during the early part of her third year of treatment, Rachel confessed to me that she was missing the opportunity of "putting Nathan down" since he was so cooperative these days. This confession and her associations to it helped Rachel to face how really furious, competitive, and envious she was of Nathan and of most men. She had dreams in which she experienced her vagina as a wound, almost as if she had been castrated. In addition, she had several fantasies of being a boy or a man, including one in which she was being circumcised by me. Analysis of this last fantasy helped Rachel see that she wanted me to help her become a boy and start life all over again as a Jewish boy.

The more Rachel confronted her rage and competition with boys and men, particularly her strong wish to be a Jewish male, the more loving and relaxed she became with Nathan and with their daughters. Intimacy and love were becoming more dominant patterns in the Abramowitz household.

The longer I worked with Rachel, the more I saw an optimism and spiritedness in her. She was investing a lot in her analysis and all of her relationships. As I thought more about this observation, I recognized it as a quality I have noted in almost all of the Orthodox Jews with whom I have worked. Rabbi Harold Kushner (1993), in his book *To Life: A Celebration of Jewish Being and Thinking*, refers several times to this strong investment in bettering the here and now as a characteristic of all observant Jews.

Although Orthodox Jews invest a great deal of themselves in their relationships, their God, and their Judaism, many of them question aspects of their Orthodoxy. Rachel was no exception.

Questions on Judaism

For the next five months Rachel spent a great deal of time in her sessions, and in between them, questioning many dimensions of her Orthodox Jewish life. When this occurred in Rachel's treatment, I knew it was normal for any Orthodox Jew. If psychotherapy, particularly dynamically oriented therapy, is essentially an examination of one's life—values, ideals, internal and external admonitions, wishes, fantasies, memories, defenses, and conflicts—then, for the observant Jew, a failure to examine his or her religious life, particularly how it is experienced subjectively, would make the therapy an abysmal failure because a major chunk of the individual's life would go unexamined.

Rachel sporadically revealed in her early phases of treatment that she had a lot of resentment being a rebbitzin. Now, after three years of treatment, she could talk about her irritations with more conviction and within an atmosphere that appeared safe to her. "I think you know by now that I feel like an appendage, being a rabbi's wife. I don't really have an identity of my own. I'm supposed to smile nicely, greet people warmly, and behave as if everything is okay," stated Rachel emphatically in a session during this period. As she elaborated on this theme, that is, having to act and seem to believe that everything in her life was all right when it wasn't, I reminded Rachel that this was the way she behaved with me in the early part of her therapy. Everything was "nice" or "all right."

Rachel responded to my comment by pointing out that during her childhood and teenage years she wondered if it was one of the ten commandments to say and act as if "everything is all right." Rachel concluded that she had been participating in a charade as she enacted the roles of the cantor's well-behaved daughter and her mother's quiet but efficient helper. She could now see better than ever before why her past and present seemed so similar. She was making them almost identical. A rebbitzin, as she saw it, was really a compliant little girl with no ego identity and a weak self-image.

As Rachel faced her subordinate position as the rabbi's wife and became less frightened of her aggression, she took on more leadership positions in and out of the synagogue, spoke up on several occasions with family and friends, and even disagreed with Nathan and other men about political issues and other matters. It was at this time she enrolled in a part-time doctoral program in American history.

What also had bothered Rachel a great deal, but which she had not discussed in much detail until now, was how the Orthodox Jewish woman was "supposed to act sexually. In Judaism menstruation is really 'a curse'; you can't have sex before it, during it, and after it," she said with intense sarcasm. "Then when your husband satisfies you sexually, he calls it a mitzvah, as if you are some charity case! Also, they look at you as so dirty you have to bathe after you've been cursed."

Toward the end of her third year of therapy, Rachel had a dream in which she was examining Nathan's penis and yelling at him, *"Traif, traif, traif!"* [unkosher] Analysis of the dream revealed that Rachel was doing to Nathan what she felt had been done to her and her sexuality. Just as she felt under inspection constantly, with her genitals condemned, so she wanted to do to Nathan in the dream. With intense rage, Rachel asserted, "I'd love to put him in his place. I've always been put in my place."

As Rachel reflected more on some of her difficulties in being an observant Jewish woman, she talked more about her mother. "My mother never stood up to my father, and all of us girls in the family have come out just like Momma. The most emotion I ever saw my mother show was when she slapped my face because I had my first menstrual period. Yeah, it was an important Jewish ritual that all mothers have to do with their daughters, but as I think of it now, it was as if all of the bitterness she had in being my father's servant and being a woman came out in that slap."

Examining her relationship with her mother further, Rachel recalled that for a good part of her life, she became nauseated every time she had to drink milk. For many years she thought that rather than this being an aversion to milk, she was obeying a dietary law. However, Rachel could now see that milk was associated with her mother and by avoiding milk, she was avoiding taking in mother's "poison" (Klein 1957). Rachel then recalled that although most of her friends found it difficult to fast on Yom Kippur and at at other times, fasting for her was a relief. It was psychologically equivalent to getting away from her mother and her mother's food, which she felt was unpalatable.

As the fourth year of Rachel's treatment was beginning, she started raising questions about God and to Him. Rachel compared herself to Tevye in the musical *Fiddler on the Roof*, who continually asked, "God, God, I work and pray so hard, why don't you make my life better?" Rachel had additional questions. They were, "God, I have been such an obedient girl. I've always been a good daughter, sister, wife, and mother. Why isn't there more joy in my life?" Or, "God, you believe in justice, mercy, and fair play. Why do you permit so much discrimination against the Jewish woman?" And, "God, do you think you could help one more Jewish woman? You helped one become a prime minister of Israel!"

As Rachel asked God to grant some of her wishes, she found herself saying, "And God, if you grant my prayers, I'll be a very good daughter." She then could see for herself how she was once again turning herself into a compliant, good daughter, and turning her fate over to the omnipotent Father in Heaven. This insight was very helpful to Rachel. Reflectively she said, "I guess everybody makes God what he or she wants to make of Him.

As long as I'm a helpless girl, I'll make Him Mr. Wonderful."

During this phase of treatment Rachel acted out some of her defiance toward God and Judaism. At a seminar her husband was conducting, he interpreted something from the Torah and ended by saying "God always loves you"; Rachel belligerently inquired out loud, "How do you know?" Everyone, particularly Nathan, was very embarrassed and the silence that ensued was very uncomfortable. On another occasion, when one of her daughters complained about walking to the synagogue on the Sabbath when it was raining, Rachel rebelliously arranged for her to take a taxi.

When Rachel was acting out her defiance toward Jewish rituals and practices, she managed to attract a lot of attention. As she found herself being discussed derogatively by congregants of the synagogue, Rachel at first feigned indifference. When Nathan became irritated at her rebelliousness, she became quite belligerent toward him. However, after she related a dream in which she arranged for me to admonish her for her recalcitrance, I could then help Rachel slowly become aware of her wish to be punished. Rachel could eventually see that her acting out her rage toward God and Judaism was linked to her hostility toward both of her parents and, to a lesser extent, toward her siblings. Just as God did not answer her prayers, so neither of her parents was particularly attentive to her emotional life. And, just as she did not receive much pleasure in being a girl in a religious Jewish home, Rachel felt discriminated against in the synagogue. As she entered her fifth year of treatment, Rachel was appearing like an adolescent, trying to find her own identity, giving up some traditional values and ideals, finding new ones, attempting to be more autonomous, without being as vitriolic. Some of these issues had to be resolved in her transference relationship with me.

The Negative Transference

Clinicians who have worked with religious patients have probably observed the same phenomenon with many of them. When these patients summon the courage to examine the metapsychology of their religious life, that is, the structural (id wishes, ego defenses, superego admonitions), the genetic (how their history and development contribute), the topographic (what unconscious forces are at work), and the dynamic (the interplay of psychic forces), this is usually followed by a great deal of resentment toward the therapist. This negative transference is inevitable for many reasons. First, the therapist is viewed as the one who has disrupted an important dynamic equilibrium and therefore is very much resented. Second, the rebellion against religious practices and rituals is usually a displacement of rebellious feelings and fantasies toward parental introjects—hence the therapist who is continually available is a most convenient target. Finally, most dynamically oriented clinicians try to encourage their patients to resolve their internal conflicts by analyzing them as they manifest themselves in the transference (Freud 1912).

Rachel, after examining and questioning Orthodox Judaism, began to examine and question psychotherapy. She thought perhaps psychoanalysis was like a religion whose tenets could not be proved. She further asserted that in psychotherapy many beliefs are imposed on the patient and maybe they weren't "wholesome" beliefs.

Further, she read that "all shrinks are *mishugenah*" (crazy). At this time it did not take much effort on my part to help Rachel talk about her resentments toward me. "Yes," she bellowed, "you are just out to get me to behave in a way that you believe is correct. My father and mother wanted me to be a compliant Jewish girl and you want me to be a compliant patient. What the hell is the difference?"

Rachel was experiencing me as a selfish, egocentric parental figure who did not have much concern with her unique life. As she vented a great deal of scorn at me, she was sure that at any moment I would retaliate and either throw her out of treatment or, if not that, yell and scream at her. Similar to the way she tried to provoke Nathan and the members of the synagogue, she attempted to upset me. She came late for several sessions, arranged to have long silences during them, bounced a few checks, mocked my voice, and made sarcastic remarks about my clothes and my office decor.

Although I knew that what Rachel was doing in her therapy was a necessary phase of the treatment, and despite the fact that I could feel much empathy for and identification with her, there was something about her belligerence that ignited some belligerence in me. As I studied my countertransference reactions, I began to have associations to some punitive women in my past, particularly to a social-work supervisor who had a name similar to Rachel's. Slowly it dawned on me that I was afraid to acknowledge that the hostility that Rachel was venting toward me in sessions was the hostility I wanted to vent toward certain mother figures but was too frightened to do so. Thus, I was secretly admiring Rachel for her spunkiness but felt guilty about doing so.

My analysis of my countertransference difficulty helped me become sensitized to Rachel's maternal transference to me. I was the mother who gave her very little and whose limitations she had to tolerate even though I infuriated her.

Rachel's negative maternal transference served a purpose that was not clear to us for some time. By making me her mother and therefore a woman, she was castrating me. Again her strong hatred for herself as a female emerged, and she had many fantasies of her mother castrating her. In one of her dreams at this time she was wearing a tallith and had me wearing a long dress—a reversal of roles.

Despite Rachel's spending several months hating me, she was "at an all-time high" in her life. Her relationship with Nathan was very good, she was enjoying h᷂ 'aughters, and felt much freer in her interpersonal life. She was making much progress in her doctoral studies, and her self-esteem and self confidence had increased.

Working Through and Termination

During most of her fifth year of treatment, Rachel began to synthesize the gains she had made in treatment. She really was able to appreciate and then modify her stance as a compliant daughter. She realized that her fear of her aggression kept her compliant and made her feel small. She was more able to differentiate between hatred and normal assertiveness.

As Rachel saw herself less as a little girl, she could enjoy herself more as a sexual woman. Her sex life with Nathan was much improved, and interpersonally she enjoyed herself more with him. Judaism became a more pleasurable dimension of her life as she felt less oppressed by and in more control of it. Rituals and practices were enacted with less anxiety and compulsiveness and with more pleasure and spontaneity.

Rachel spent about four months working on termination of treatment. At times I was experienced as the good mother whom she did not want to leave. I was also viewed as a rejecting mother who was throwing her out. In addition, I was the ideal man, with whom she could be happy in marriage. However, when this fantasy was punctured, I emerged as a mean father figure and a rejecting brother.

One of Rachel's strongest resistances at termination was her wish to have a continued relationship with me. She fantasied us meeting for coffee or being on a panel together in a university setting, or having me appear as a guest speaker at her husband's synagogue. As these fantasies were analyzed, they were clearly derivatives of her wish to be my daughter, and I would be a combination of good mother and father.

It was not easy for Rachel to relinquish her wishes to hold on to me. For a long time she seemed more interested in planning reunions than in working toward separation and increased autonomy. However, she could see that I was quite firm in wanting to analyze her requests rather than gratify them. In response she had one of her angriest tirades in what was close to a six-year treatment relationship. She told me, "You are helping me continue my war with men. Since you are probably a Jewish man (she was never quite sure), I think you have an investment in being my enemy."

Eventually Rachel could own her desire to continue her war with Jewish men and other wars in which she had been engaged. She ended her treatment recognizing that if she didn't choose the path of being a servile, masochistic rebbitzin, she did not have to be a warrior. She could work and love with pleasure.

4

A
Born-Again
Orthodox Jew

It was 7:30 in the morning. I was drinking my usual cup of coffee in my office and leisurely reading the *New York Times* when the phone rang. This is one of the few times during a busy day that my phone normally does not ring, and I was relishing this private time before I saw my first patient.

Feeling some annoyance at having my peace intruded on, I picked up the phone and the voice at the other end blurted out, "Are you a shrink?" My annoyance grew but, trying to keep my cool, I asked, "May I know with whom I'm speaking?" "Yeah, I'll tell you," the voice replied. It was a man's voice and I guessed he was about 30 years old. He seemed quite provocative and rather belligerent and his gruffness frightened me a bit. He went on, "My doctor said I need a shrink and he gave me your name. He told me there was nothing wrong with my body but I need

a shrink. By the way, how much do you soak people for?"
I then asked, "Perhaps you'd like to come in and meet me
and we can talk about fees and some of your other
concerns?" My caller asked, "Well, how do you know you
can help me?" I answered, "I don't know if I can. Maybe
if we meet we can try to determine that together."

Irritated at the caller for getting in touch with me at an
inopportune time, I began to realize I was feeling very
skeptical about him. I wondered to myself, "If we do make
an appointment, will he show up?" He sounded more like
an angry foreman arrogantly speaking to a lowly super-
visee than a prospective patient asking for therapeutic
help.

Just as I realized that my caller had not given me his
name, he said, "By the way, Herbert, my name is Meyer
Stein. I'll try you out. Yeah, give me an appointment!"
Instead, I politely asked him what would be a convenient
time and day for him to have a consultation. Although we
had difficulty finding a mutually convenient time to get
together, eventually we were able to do so. We made an
appointment for three days later.

I thought about my phone conversation with Meyer
Stein several times. Not only did I realize that I had a
strong resistance to meeting with him, but I found myself
preparing for combat. I felt as if I were getting ready for a
boxing match or a tense debate. As I reflected further on
my conversation with Meyer Stein, I had several peculiar
reactions. First, I wondered how come I was thinking so
much about this man before meeting him, yet concomitantly saying to myself I did not want to meet him.
Obviously I was terribly ambivalent. Second, although my
prospective patient's name was a Jewish one, as I pictured
him he reminded me of an anti-Semitic boy from my
childhood whose name was Ross. Ross was twice my size

and whenever he would taunt me and make his derogatory anti-Semitic remarks, I was so terrified of him that I suppressed my aggression and felt helpless. Rarely, if ever, did I turn a prospective patient into an enemy before I even met him! I was doing this with Meyer Stein and knew that I would have to work hard to monitor and master my counterresistances, particularly my countertransference reactions (Strean 1993a). I did not answer to my satisfaction why I had such intense and conflicted feelings toward him.

The First Interview

When I entered my waiting room I saw a tall, bearded man, about six feet tall, who was in his late twenties. He was wearing a yarmulke and had on unpressed brown trousers, a rather dirty sweater, and a shirt that looked as if it hadn't been laundered during six months of wear.

When I introduced myself, the gentleman looked away but got up from the chair in the waiting room. I invited him to follow me into the office. When I showed him the chair he would be sitting in, he did not sit down but instead took off his sweater and threw it on the floor. He then looked at a picture of Freud on my wall and provocatively inquired, "You are a Freudian, huh?" I responded, "Does that concern you?" "Oh, one of those," Meyer retorted. "Answer a question with a question!" Then he snarled at me and a long silence followed.

I interrupted the silence by saying, "We're having some difficulty getting to know each other." "Oh, no, we aren't," said Meyer. He went on, "You are having difficulty. You can't answer questions now and you didn't over the phone." Then he took his shoes off and threw them next to his sweater.

When I suggested to Meyer that I seemed to be making it tough for him, he responded, "Look, I know all about you guys. I've been to four shrinks already and I know all of you do not want to answer questions. You hide behind your professional garb and you don't give much!"

Hearing Meyer's very unsuccessful experiences with therapists and sensing his intense antipathy toward them and now to me, I commented, "With the unpleasant experiences you've had with therapists, I'm not sure why you want to see me." Meyer liked my comment and replied, "Oh, you're not a money grubber. You try to understand. That's not bad."

When Meyer recognized that he had uttered something positive to me, he seemed to regret it. He then went on to say, "You guys will do anything for a buck. Even sound as if you care!" I then asked Meyer, "Did the therapists you worked with seem not to care about you?" "That's putting it mildly," Meyer responded. With a great deal of indignation he said, "All of them had their own prejudices and biases against Orthodox Judaism. You see, I became an Orthodox Jew a couple of years ago after having lived in a home with infidels. My mother and father had limited use for God, the synagogue, or for kindness, and I decided to make something of myself. All those shrinks tried to talk me out of my beliefs. They were hypocrites themselves and not compassionate."

Despite my sensing that Meyer was what the psychoanalyst Bergler (1969) called "an injustice collector," and therefore quite paranoid, I began to feel that underneath his suspicions, arrogance, anger, and contempt was a frightened, vulnerable boy who was yearning to be understood. As he talked about his previous therapists being uncompassionate, I couldn't be sure how much of what he stated was the product of distortion and how much these therapists did in fact fail to approach his newly found religious life in a neutral way. I thought I'd test this out and see what Meyer would do if I attempted to demonstrate some understanding of his religious life. I asked, "What did your previous therapists fail to appreciate about your religious life?" Meyer looked at me with some surprise in his eyes but said, with some skepticism in his manner, "They didn't see I was groping to find some meaning in life. They were more interested in telling me I was neurotic and how I should live my life. That's the trouble with you guys. You think you know all the answers."

As I kept quiet, Meyer went on to tell me more about his unhappy life. He was a skilled computer analyst but got into arguments with bosses and peers and went from job to job, not lasting anywhere more than a year. What was true of his therapeutic and professional life was also true of his relationships with women and, "for that matter, people in general." Often he was sexually impotent. As he described his inability to sustain relationships with women, he showed some sadness for the first time in the interview. With a tear or two and choking back more tears, he said, "I've never met a woman who I thought cared about me." In addition to his very problematic interpersonal life, Meyer shared with me that he had frequent nightmares in which he was being physically hurt after being chased by mobs. Also, he had often had migraine headaches, gastrointestinal problems, and asthma since he was 5 years old.

Meyer informed me that he had two younger sisters, one three years younger and the other five years younger than he. According to Meyer, his "cold and angry" parents

preferred girls to boys and he always felt like "an un-
wanted child." Although he was always a good student,
majoring in mathematics in college, he was usually a loner
throughout most of his twenty-nine years.

Meyer agreed to see me twice a week "as an experi-
ment." He had no problem agreeing to the fee I requested
and left saying, "I'll give it a try."

After Meyer left my office, I could better understand
some of my reactions to the phone conversation with him.
To handle strong feelings of vulnerability, self-loathing,
and a readiness to be rejected, Meyer seemed to go on the
offensive and tried to make the other person feel vulnerable and self-hating. He had succeeded in many ways
with me during the phone conversation and many times
during the early part of the consultation, he came close to
succeeding again. But I was beginning to empathize with
the emotionally battered child in him and felt that if I
could keep my cool and respect his coping mechanisms,
particularly his views on religion, maybe I could help him.
I certainly wanted to try.

The Battle Begins

Although Meyer seemed to leave his first interview in a
relatively calm mood, by the second session he was on the
warpath. Again, he took off his shoes, tossed them on the
floor with his sweater and provocatively ordered, "You
begin!" I responded, "Okay," which seemed to shock him.
Obviously he wanted to fight with me and I frustrated him
by my willingness to comply with his request. He then
looked at me in silence but with an air of suspicion. I broke
the silence by asking, "How did you feel coming over here

today?" With much anger Meyer yelled, "Look, I told *you* to begin, damn it! Don't ask me a question! Make a statement!" I said, "Okay, I'll make a statement. This is the statement: I'm wondering how you were feeling coming here today." Meyer laughed scornfully and said, "Touché." Then he asked me, "How do you think I felt coming here today?" I answered, "Ready to have a fight with me!"

Meyer then told me I was the one who wanted to fight. He was interested in knowing what my investment was in arguing with him. He was clearly reversing roles (A. Freud 1946), becoming the therapist and making me the patient, exploring my motives for fighting. Although I was reasonably clear that Meyer was projecting his wishes to fight onto me and trying to disown his hostility, I felt that I would not be helpful to him if I exposed his defensiveness. Therefore, as if he were a child, I encouraged him to be the doctor and have him make interpretations about my wish to argue and fight.

For the next seven sessions Meyer spent most of his time analyzing me. He told me that I was probably a very insecure man who became a therapist in order to feel superior to people and to order them around. Stated Meyer, "Without this defense of yours, you'd feel like a fragile good-for-nothing." Meyer further suggested that I'd had a traumatic childhood and that was what piqued my interest in "the child" in my patients.

In these sessions Meyer looked straight at me much like a teacher who was instructing a child. Sometimes he would venture hypotheses about my family background. "You probably had an authoritarian father and a weak mother. You seem to show both traits," concluded Meyer somewhat dogmatically.

By Meyer's tenth session he was neither analyzing me nor arguing with me. Indirectly he implied that because I was able to take his criticisms without retaliating, he was feeling a little safer with me. Feeling in less danger, Meyer went on to talk about his own life a bit. He spoke about both of his parents being "like refrigerators" and offering him almost no warmth. Whenever he tried to show his hurt or anger to his parents, they did not seem to be emotionally available. He was beginning to realize that he viewed "most of the world and most people as refrigerators."

No sooner was I beginning to feel that Meyer and I were forming a therapeutic alliance (Greenson 1967) than Meyer proved otherwise. It was about the third month of treatment when Meyer came in and asked, "Are we getting anywhere?" I wondered what he thought and again he was furious with me for asking him to explore his own thoughts and feelings. He told me that talk was cheap and he didn't feel I could help him very much nor had I up until now. However, he reported his first dream at this time. In the dream he was in a psychology class and was actively listening to the instructor who "seemed to be a nice guy." Because the instructor appeared to be one who would respond positively to his queries and comments, Meyer ventured a question. "However," Meyer pointed out, "what seemed to be a pleasant dream turned out to be a nightmare. The instructor, instead of listening to my question, started to yell at me and before I knew it, we were shoving and ready to clobber each other."

Meyer told me that the dream reflected his "clear perception of so-called experts in psychology." They start off being nice guys but they really do want to fight. Although it was tempting for me to tell Meyer that inasmuch as he arranged the dream, it could be inferred that he had a wish to fight with psychologists, I knew by now that his paranoia was intense and pervasive and that if I suggested he take some responsibility for his fights, he would just fight some more. Therefore, I told Meyer that I thought the dream reflected his distrust of me and psychologists. I start off nice but I end up a fighter.

Meyer appeared unthreatened by my interpretation and went on to tell me he wished he could trust me. Then he could share his Orthodox Jewish interests with me and let me in on such personal matters as women, sex, politics, and fantasies. "But," Meyer warned, "as long as you are eager to be aggressive I have to be cautious with you."

Although Meyer was in a combative mode, I felt by his manner and tone that he now had some interest in constructively communicating with me. Therefore I went back to his dream and suggested that if we look at it a little more carefully, it suggests that there was something about a warm peaceful interchange that bothers me. In the dream I disrupted that and began to argue and shove.

Meyer began to analyze me again. He told me I was an insecure fellow, quite effeminate, and that to protect myself I went on the offensive. I suggested, "Then I'm afraid to show you my vulnerabilities." Meyer then showed me how sharp he was. He said, "Look, Herbert, you think you are pulling something off on me! Don't be mistaken. If you talk about your vulnerabilities and think of showing them to me, don't think I'll show you mine!"

As I listened to Meyer's thoughts about who was going to show what to whom, and who was going to do it first, I was reminded of the children's game of "I'll show you if you show me." In effect, it is a sexual game to see who has more confidence in getting undressed first. Meyer, in effect, was fighting off a homosexual transference and had to make sure he would not reveal too much to me. Otherwise, he would feel he was getting undressed in front of me. Interpretations from me seemed to be experienced by him as phallic penetrations (Fenichel 1945). Consequently, I had to be careful that I was not "too hard" on him.

As I continued to respect Meyer's resistance to close involvement with me (Strean 1990), he became less paranoid, more communicative, and a little more revealing. He stopped throwing his shoes and sweater on the floor and showed more composure in his demeanor.

By the end of six months of twice-a-week sessions, Meyer seemed more committed to therapy with me. He had sustained a computer operator's job for more than five months, he was dating women and fighting less with them, and was taking an active part in educational and social activities at his synagogue.

Meyer Thinks I Am an Anti-Semite

A constant theme in Meyer's therapy until now and for most of the duration of treatment was that after Meyer felt closer to me, he would have to find fault with me. He desperately needed his paranoid defense to ward off warm and/or homoerotic fantasies. Therefore, soon after sharing with me that his life was going better, particularly his religious life at the synagogue, he took up arms again.

During his eighth month of therapy, Meyer queried, "The doctor that referred me to you said that he thought you were Jewish. Are you?" I responded, "Meyer, I'd like to tell you about my religious affiliation but I don't think that if I do that right now it'll help our work. Judaism is a very important issue in your life and what your impressions are of me as a Jew or non-Jew are more important right now than the facts." I was not shocked that Meyer was very irritated with my response. "I've told you all along that you are scared to level with me. You don't want to tell me that you are against religion, against my strong beliefs in God and the Torah, and that you are probably an agnostic anti-Semite," Meyer said with extreme exasperation. I asked Meyer, "What if these were true of me?" "Well, if the truth be told, you are afraid of losing a patient. You know damn well you are in this for the money and you want to keep me!" commented Meyer with much derision.

We were now in the seventh month of therapy and Meyer brought in his second dream. In the dream he went to a house of prostitution. In the bedroom with the prostitute, she made fun of him. She was scornful of his circumcised penis, laughed at his beard, and scoffed at his yarmulke. As Meyer was about to leave the prostitute's room, she grabbed him and said, "Look, stay, I need your money. I'll give you a blow job."

Not immediately but later on, Meyer was able to acknowledge that the dream was "a transference dream." (He called it that because it would help him avoid the anxiety that was stirred up by the sexual intimacy that he wanted with me, but shunned.) At first, he pointed out the similarity between a prostitute and a therapist. "They both act as if they care about you, but all they want is your money." When I saw that he had some conviction of his own that he had made me the woman prostitute, I asked Meyer what his associations were about my demeaning his identity as a Jew. With more insight than he had shown to date, Meyer calmly reflected, "You see, Doc, being Jewish gives me a feeling of potency. The yarmulke makes me feel my head is bigger, my beard makes me feel my face is longer, and my big cock assures me that I'm a big man." I could then tell Meyer that when I mock his

Jewish identity in the dream, I am really castrating him. Meyer concurred and went on to tell me that although he wasn't positive I was a goy (a gentile), I often acted like one. Therefore, I resented the fact that Meyer was "a member of the tribe," one of God's chosen people, and envious of "the many privileges and pleasures that are always part of an elite status."

Though Meyer was only in the ninth month of treatment, I had the distinct impression that he and I were now examining and discussing the crux of his difficulties. He could now see that the many power struggles in which he was consistently involved had to do with what we were currently working on in therapy. Meyer was becoming quite clear about the etiology of his interpersonal conflicts. If he didn't castrate, he would be castrated. If he didn't hit out, he'd be hit.

We were able to gain further understanding of his power struggles, particularly as they impinged on his Jewish identity. Prior to his becoming a religious Jew at the age of 26, Meyer confided that he felt like "a wimp," that is, castrated. To feel more virile, he began wearing a beard, a yarmulke, and other "extensions" such as a Star of David. If he didn't have these extensions, he felt "like a nobody." Nonetheless, he was always afraid that his extensions would be taken away, but he didn't know why anyone would want to do that. Trying to answer this question took up much of the next six months of treatment.

"Why I Became a Jew"

After Meyer had been in therapy a little over a year and was very much involved in analyzing himself, particularly the dynamics of his becoming a religious Jew, I suggested that we get together more often. To my surprise and without much resistance on his part, Meyer agreed that it would be "a good idea." He took the position that more therapy would make him a better Jew and that was his top priority. Becoming a better Jew meant that he would be more "insightful," more "sensitive to the souls of my brethren," and less "hostile." He further suggested that psychotherapy made him feel more learned and that was also part of being a good Jew.

When Meyer began coming three times a week, I noticed that he would periodically gaze at the couch. After he had done this a few times, I asked him about his interest in the couch. The sarcastic Meyer asserted himself and he said with disdain something that also had validity, "Come on, Doc" (I was now a doctor, albeit a truncated one, "Doc" instead of Herbert), Meyer admonished, "don't be so coy. Be direct. Why don't you say, 'Take the couch'?" Although Meyer and I were both being coy (because we both were resisting a more intimate relationship), I had to subject my resistance to examination first. I said to Meyer, "I'm not sure why I'm being coy about your using the couch. Do you have any ideas?" Meyer, again with some accuracy, said, "Maybe you are afraid of what will come out. Maybe I'll talk about stuff that'll make you anxious." "Like what?" I asked. "Oh, maybe I'll talk about incest, murder, homosexuality, and you'll get upset."

The way our dialogue regarding the couch progressed was quite fascinating and unconventional. Meyer kept trying to reassure me that the idea was really not too "threatening or traumatic" for either of us and "we should go ahead." (I felt that I was a virgin being reassured that our contemplated affair would not destroy me!)

Meyer appeared quite comfortable on the couch. He

had many memories, shared some fantasies, worked on dreams, and was able to analyze different dimensions of the transference with me. He was a full-fledged analytic patient by the eighteenth month of treatment.

One of Meyer's early dreams during this new phase of treatment was one in which he was converting me to Judaism. His manner of converting me was interesting. In the dream I was naked. He was washing me with soap and water and ministering to me very tenderly. Then he startled me and took a knife from behind his back and attempted to circumcise me. As he tried to cut off part of my penis, I ran away.

We spent several sessions analyzing Meyer's dream. In circumcising me, he was, of course, also castrating me. He "had to castrate" me before I castrated him. Just as he was quite sure that while I was behind the couch I might do something violent that would startle him, he protected himself by doing that to me first. Eventually we were able to get to the homosexual elements of the dream. Meyer, for the first time, talked about how he yearned for tender love and care from a mother and father, but felt that both of his parents opposed giving it to him. Consequently, every time he wanted love, he was in a fight with mother and father. In the dream, we again reversed roles and he was giving to me what he wanted—warmth, tenderness, kindness, and touching—things he wanted but which seemed very forbidden to him.

Analysis of the dream led to a prolonged discussion of why Meyer had become a "born-again Jew." As a Jew, particularly an Orthodox Jew, he would not only feel like a virile man for the first time, but he would receive from God all of the love that he wanted from his parents but had never received. His fellow congregants in the synagogue became warm siblings and the synagogue was a warm home. He was "born again."

In talking about his motives for "becoming more Jewish," Meyer referred back to the dream in which I was nude. Insightfully he remarked, "You were the baby I'd like to be."

In reviewing some more of his motives for becoming an Orthodox Jew, Meyer was able to furnish me with more understanding of his psychosexual development. For example, when we took a look at his constant nausea and stomach aches, many of Meyer's strong cannibalistic fantasies came to the fore. In response to a very ungiving mother, Meyer was very critical of his strong appetite for all kinds of food that "were bad." Kosher food and obeying other dietary laws curbed his strong oral wishes and also helped Meyer not to suffer so many gastrointestinal problems.

During his second year of treatment, as he faced his oral drives, Meyer's gastrointestinal problems diminished. Particularly when he made me the feeding mother in the transference and had fantasies of sucking at my breasts and merging with me, by facing his symbiotic desires he was able better to tolerate his real appetite for food. Although he realized that his preoccupation with kosher food and dietary laws served as a protection against his cannibalistic desires, he maintained his regimen in obeying dietary laws, pointing out that by so doing he felt "close to my people."

Meyer frequently contrasted the warm kitchen in the synagogue with Mother's "cold breasts." Now that he was dating, he told me that he was very much interested in Jewish women who had big breasts.

When Meyer further reflected on his early childhood,

he not only angrily mentioned that he was never breast-fed nor warmly held by either parent, but he also described early and arbitrary toilet training. His mother, he informed me, frequently bragged to friends and relatives that all of her children were toilet trained by the time they were 1 year old. Meyer, in response to this, became "sloppy," and "didn't give a damn about showers or baths."

Despite the fact that Meyer continued "to be a slob," and "enjoyed it in many ways," he was very careful to remind me several times that whenever he went to the synagogue or social or educational events under Jewish sponsorship, he was always dressed in a "clean suit with a clean shirt." He reminded me that in Judaism "cleanliness is next to Godliness." He also mentioned that if he thought I were a practicing Jew, he would come better dressed to the sessions.

As Meyer became more aware of his "wish to shit all over others," particularly his desire to defy me and "mess up" my office by throwing his sweater and shoes "all over the place," he began to come to his sessions less disheveled but not particularly well groomed. "As long as this is not a House of Worship I don't have to worry about getting dressed up," Meyer mused.

Occasionally, while Meyer lay on the couch, his yarmulke would fall off. I knew he was becoming less paranoid when he said on more than one of these occasions, "I would have blamed you for this a year or so ago, but now I know it's the law of gravity."

Sexual Issues

Toward the end of Meyer's third year of therapy, he spent a lot of time discussing his sexual problems and fantasies. He was able to acknowledge that Judaism, by keeping women in a rigid subordinate role, gave him much security. In the synagogue and elsewhere, when he observed the Jewish women confined to a specific place, "this kind of segregation" pleased him.

As we analyzed Meyer's segregationist philosophy, it became clear that underneath his male chauvinism were fantasies of being a girl. He talked at length of his envy of his two younger sisters, both of whom he was convinced were favored by both parents. Meyer realized that just as he did not have too much to do with his sisters, he found the separation of women from men in the synagogue "like old home week."

Meyer also reported that prior to becoming an Orthodox Jew at the age of 26, his sex life was "very neurotic." Most of the time he was very shy and inhibited with young women. However, when he did get together with them he was frequently impotent or ejaculated before entry. He became humiliated by his poor performance when having sex with "nice women" and began to go to prostitutes. Although he could perform better sexually when with prostitutes, he felt demeaned and disgusted that he "had to pay to get love," much as he felt with me when he began therapy.

With much courage, Meyer could confess to me that one of the reassuring parts of being an Orthodox Jew was his being "required by law" to avoid sex with women. Then he did not "have to feel like a failure."

Meyer was able to appreciate the defensive function that his sexual abstinence from women provided when he began to discuss his compulsive masturbation and masturbatory fantasies. Meyer had been masturbating at least twice a day ever since he was 12 years old and continued at this same frequency up to this time in treatment, when he was 33 years old. In his masturbatory fantasies he would frequently whip the woman with whom he was having sex. Often he chose women who were actresses; on other occasions he fantasied having sex with women who were pictured in *Playboy* magazines.

As we attempted to understand better Meyer's masturbatory fantasies, we learned a great deal inasmuch as whipping women in his fantasies was an overdetermined issue. First, it was his way of "hitting out and expressing revenge" toward his sisters and mother. Second, by using a whip he could feel "strong and powerful" and beat the women into submission. Third, inasmuch as he was involved in a power struggle in sex and feared castration, his long whip was reassuring. Finally, Meyer was involved in much phallic-oedipal competition when he had sex with mother and sister substitutes. Consequently, he anticipated retaliation for his hostile wishes. Keeping a whip drove away his enemies.

While discussing his sexual life, Meyer moved into a fairly strong homosexual transference toward me. He had numerous fantasies of sucking my penis and "extracting the juices" to give him strength. He also fantasied having anal intercourse with me and enjoyed the closeness as well as the hardness of my penis. This, too, gave him a feeling of strength, believing at times that he had incorporated my penis and made it his own. Also, Meyer had fantasies of being a woman with me and having a baby.

As Meyer was able to make his homosexual wishes more conscious and accept them with less anxiety, he had more energy at his disposal to put into more constructive and less defensive use. By the end of his fourth year of therapy, he was dating one woman who was Jewish (but not Orthodox), enjoying her very much, and having mutually satisfactory sex. He had kept his same job and now had a supervisory position. His income had increased and so had his self-confidence and self-image. As I was thinking he was nearing the end of his therapy, Meyer surprised me with a strong shift in his attitude toward his therapy and me.

A Treatment Crisis

As Meyer was entering his fifth year of treatment, he brought in a dream in which he was in heaven and in psychoanalysis with God. At first, I thought to myself that he was making me God and having a grandiose fantasy that involved both of us. But as he associated more to the dream, it appeared that he was getting away from me and becoming closer to God. This was confirmed in a session when he modified Psalm 23 and instead of saying, "The Lord is my shepherd, I shall not want," he said with only mild sarcasm, "The Lord is my therapist, I shall not want."

Further associations to the dream by Meyer made me conclude that he was now in a strong negative transference. He was behaving the way he had when he first began treatment. "You are a fraud and a fake. I thought I could trust you but I can't!" Meyer vehemently asserted. He went on to accuse me of trying to take his Orthodox Judaism away from him and turn him into a "Freudian believer." Meyer was quite convinced that I had seduced him into a way of life that was my "religion" and that I had been trying to convert him to Freudianism from Judaism.

At first, Meyer's revived paranoia stumped me. But as I thought about it theoretically, I knew that paranoia invariably defended against unacceptable homosexuality. Yet,

Meyer was able to bring out many of his homosexual fantasies. So what was going on?

As I listened carefully to Meyer's associations, it slowly became clear that he was feeling like a disappointed lover with me. Just as he had hoped that Judaism would lead him back to the Garden of Eden and provide a paradise for him, this is what he fantasied psychotherapy would also provide. I had failed Meyer by being an "imperfect, limited" parent and he felt disillusioned with psychotherapy and thus furious with me.

At this point in the treatment, Meyer compared me with his father who, because he was a competent accountant, "made me think he would be a good father." Stated Meyer, "Well, Strean, just because you appear on the surface to be a competent therapist doesn't mean you are a kind man." He began to recall times in his childhood and teenage years when he wanted to play ball with his father who wasn't available; either he was busy doing work or was asleep. Meyer reminded me that he never had a father or father figures in his life who would listen to him and support him. He thought I was going to be that father but I let him down. Meyer's dreams expressed both his yearning for a strong father and his disillusionment with me. In a dream during this time, in which he burned down my office, Meyer then became the biblical Moses next to the burning bush and had God come down from heaven to comfort him. Meyer was able to see the meaning of the dream by himself and really did not want any help from me in interpreting it. "Burning down your office is my way of getting rid of you, and I'm burned up because you are a cold, withdrawn bastard like my father. I want to be a loved son like Moses was and I need God because neither you nor my father is available." However, as Meyer associated further to the dream, he realized that the face of God in the dream was a combination of his father's and mine, thus revealing that a God in his life would compensate for what had been lacking in his relationship with his father and me.

Associating to another dream in which he made himself Abraham and was with God again, Meyer told me that in contrast to Moses' and Abraham's interactions with God, his relationship with me was barren. Commented Meyer, "Moses and Abraham always felt that God was with them. They felt strengthened and supported by Him. You leave me alone all the time. You want me to do all the work. Instead of being an active father, you are a weak nobody who is lazy. God is not lazy and that's why I need Him."

Meyer spent most of his fifth year of treatment expressing his strong dissatisfaction, disappointment, and disillusionment with me. He recalled how many times he had felt so very alone on the couch that whatever we were working on seemed to be his job to figure out, while I contributed next to nothing. One time he compared me with Abraham, who was ready to sacrifice Isaac to God. According to Meyer I was exploiting him in order to prove that Freud was right; then I would be loved by the psychoanalytic establishment. He felt "used and abused" much more often than he felt helped.

At this point in Meyer's treatment, I felt quite attuned to the little boy in him and therefore did not become threatened by his attacks on me. Although Meyer was very demeaning of me, I could very much empathize with the crushed and disappointed child in him. I felt throughout his tirades that he knew that the suffering boy in him was not going unnoticed by me and this perception on his part, though unverbalized, nonetheless helped him to begin to see me as something more than a neglectful father and incompetent therapist.

As is true with most shifts in psychotherapy, Meyer modified his negative transference gradually. For example, in one session he declared that "not all shrinks are no good." It was the Freudian group to which I belonged that was most suspect. Meyer pointed out that Freudians think they are gods and promise a utopia. Jungians were much better and were interested in Gnosticism. This expression of increased tolerance moved toward more positive statements about psychotherapy and psychotherapists. He pointed out that some are more humane than others, that some are less hostile and more caring, and some really listen to their patients.

Meyer eventually could tell me that I had some positive qualities, too. Slowly he could acknowledge that much of his hatred toward me came from the desperation he felt in not having anyone in his life to take care of him most of the time. This made him feel weak, helpless, and incapable of negotiating for himself "in this difficult world."

Working Through and Termination

Meyer's treatment lasted six and a half years. His termination phase, I realized in hindsight, had begun after he had been in treatment for more than five years and went into the strong negative transference that I have just reviewed. He was expressing the inevitable anger that all patients feel when they are compelled to face the fact that they were never promised a rose garden, a Garden of Eden, or a paradise. It was as if Meyer was already expressing the usual sentiments of a patient ending treatment and I was behind him (in more ways than one).

As I analyzed my counterresistance, I realized that I

wanted to begin working on termination on a positive note, and without this reassurance from Meyer to me, I might feel like too much of a failure—something that Meyer wanted me to feel much of the time. Hence, I was not clear or sufficiently objective about what Meyer was experiencing at this time.

Having eventually grasped more clearly what was going on for Meyer, I could work with him more constructively toward termination. Although there were flashes of anger on his part during his termination phase, his predominant affect was one of sadness. He appeared to be in mourning, as if having to accept the death of someone he loved. With tears he confessed, "I feel like an orphan who has lost his loving parents and can't figure out if there is any way to replace them." Later he had a dream in which he was reciting the Kaddish (prayer for the dead) in the synagogue and it was clear that I was "the departed" for whom he was mourning.

I was able to help Meyer see that his dream reflected not only that he was very sad about not continuing his relationship with me, but it also revealed that he wanted me dead. Although for a while he resisted facing this wish, eventually he could get in touch with his anger. He was resentful that psychotherapy was a process that worked toward separation, not reunion. He had wishes to see me socially, perhaps by my visiting his synagogue or having a drink with him somewhere. When he realized that these wishes for contact with me were going to be frustrated, he did acknowledge some of his fury.

After Meyer and I set a date for ending our work, his anger subsided and he began calmly to review what he had accomplished in his therapy. He felt that his foremost accomplishment was becoming less furious and suspicious and much more loving and trusting. Meyer now had a steady girlfriend, Emily, and was looking forward to marrying her. He was enjoying his work, was making a good salary, and was in a leadership position there. He was not hating his parents and sisters as much, seeing them much more as they were.

Regarding his relationship to Judaism, Meyer recognized that he did not need to proselytize as much, realizing that by trying to convince others to adopt his religious beliefs, he was trying to convince himself, and was not confronting his own doubts. He became much more tolerant of others who interpreted the Torah differently from how he did, and he also became less rigid in following Orthodox dogma. Inasmuch as his fiancee, Emily, was more of a secular Jew, Meyer and she both tried to compromise on observing rituals such as traveling on the Sabbath, eating in nonkosher restaurants, and praying. Each of them tried to accommodate the other and they worked out their differences quite well.

At the end of treatment, Meyer still regarded himself as a practicing Orthodox Jew, but, as he saw it, "I'm less compulsive about it, enjoying Judaism more, and am less obsessive about God."

Approximately a year after treatment ended, Meyer married Emily and a year later they had a baby boy. In a note to me at that time, Meyer said, "I'm doing quite well."

5

The
Ardent
Feminist

The phone rang and the woman's voice at the other end provocatively stated, "I'm interested in having a consultation with you to see whether you are qualified to be my therapist." When I remained silent, the caller continued, saying, "My name is Joyce Kaplansky and I'm a social worker in a Jewish family agency. Your name was given to me by my supervisor. She said you were not a sexist therapist." After another moment of silence, Ms. Kaplansky asked, "Are you sensitive to feminist concerns?"

I had learned rather early in my clinical work that when a prospective patient asks a question about a therapist's qualifications, he or she usually has doubts about whether the therapist can be helpful. Thus I have concluded that it is usually not a good idea to answer patients' questions, but to help them talk about their doubts and concerns instead (Strean 1990). Therefore I said to Ms. Kaplansky,

"I get the feeling that you want a therapist who can relate well to your concerns as a woman. Maybe you could come in for a meeting with me in my office and see for yourself?" "I could," replied Ms. Kaplansky with some hesitation. Then she raised her voice and aggressively commented, "Look, I need a therapist who respects me for being an observant Jew and a feminist. I'm not sure you qualify."

Although I had spoken to Joyce Kaplansky for less than three minutes, I had already formed an impression of her and had some strong feelings toward her. She appeared very demanding, quite aggressive, imperious, and not very likable. I thought to myself, "I bet she has a poor track record with men, because I've said next to nothing to her and she's already inducing a wish to get away from her." The fantasy I had while on the phone with her was that she and I were lawyers, and rather hostile adversaries, at that!

Responding to Joyce Kaplansky's concern about my lack of qualifications to work with a Jewish feminist, I said, "Inasmuch as you are a social worker, you know it takes a while before a client can allow herself to trust you with important issues in her life. You may or may not be able to trust me, and I may or may not be able to help you." Joyce Kaplansky answered, "Well, you are not as dogmatic as I thought you might be." After a long pause she asked, "Do you think we should get together?" Realizing she was ambivalent about seeing me, I said, "You may want to think about it for a day or two and call me with a decision. Or you may want to make an appointment for next week, and then you can change your mind and call me if you decide not to keep the appointment." Joyce felt understood when I showed some awareness of her ambivalence. She said, "I think you show some flexibility. I think neither of us is making a big commitment if we agree to one consultation." Then Joyce jocularly commented, "He who hesitates is lost." Feeling a diminution of tension after going through a tense ordeal, I jocularly commented, "But look before you leap." Joyce laughed for a moment and then we made an appointment without difficulty.

When I entered the waiting room three days later, Joyce was there for her appointment. She was standing at the window looking out. Hearing me enter the waiting room, she turned and faced me. She was about five feet five inches, in a black dress and shoes. Although she was well groomed, the obvious frown on her face together with her unbecoming brown kerchief made her appear like a stern schoolteacher who was ready to admonish a student.

As I walked with Joyce Kaplansky to my office, I realized I had already formed a negative countertransference toward her. I had made her my seventh-grade schoolteacher, a woman who obviously had it in for boys, a teacher who didn't particularly like me. I remembered Miss Henry as a teacher who never was satisfied with anything a boy said, no matter how he said it, and regardless of its validity. The more I became aware of my countertransference reaction toward Joyce, the more inhibited I began to feel with her. As I sat down opposite her, I did not feel the usual empathy I experience toward a patient. I felt tension and resistance instead.

I was grateful to Joyce that she began the interview by telling me that the main reason she wanted therapy was because she was dissatisfied with her progress as a social worker. By this she meant that she was very disappointed with her limited salary and low status in her agency. Joyce's willingness to initiate the interview with me helped me gain some composure and I listened with interest as she told me how women are excluded from administrative positions in social work and placed in "demeaned" positions. She was "furious" that men "had everything" and she "had nothing."

Joyce continued to elaborate on the pervasiveness of sexism not only in social work but throughout society. She talked about women being a minority group in politics, business, and in many other sectors of our culture. With less anger in her voice, she thoughtfully commented, "Although I'm 31 years old, it's only been during the last two years that I have recognized the tremendous discrimination in Orthodox Judaism." She told me that women have been segregated and discriminated against and "can't rise to the top" within the Orthodox Jewish movement.

As I silently associated to Joyce's comments about women being mistreated in the important areas of her life, I could also sense her antipathy and competition toward men and wondered how much of this arose in her own family. Inasmuch as she presented herself as a victim of all kinds of institutional sexism, I also wondered how she expected me to help her with this, or if she really wanted my help with anything. I then thought I'd ask her if she had been a victim of sexism in other areas of her life. Joyce replied, "Well, I didn't like the way they treated girls at the yeshiva—we were second-class citizens. And in my home where my father was a rabbi, he obviously preferred my two brothers. By the way, I was stuck in the middle. One brother is two years older and the other is three years younger. The oldest is also a rabbi and the youngest is a businessman."

Joyce described her father as a man who was so involved in the synagogue and with communal activities that he did not have much time for his family. When he was with the family he delivered "long and impersonal lectures" at them, was frequently angry, and was a very strict disciplinarian. Mother was described as frequently sick, complaining a lot, and was very intimidated by her husband. Joyce was not particularly close to her brothers and felt quite a bit of contempt coming from them toward her.

With about fifteen minutes remaining before our interview had to end, I told Joyce that although it was very clear that she'd had to cope with a great deal of sexism most of her life, I wasn't very clear about how she thought therapy could help her. Joyce answered by telling me that she'd already had "two unsuccessful experiences with therapy." The first treatment experience occurred when she was 20 years old and a junior in college. A male sociology professor told her that she had "an axe to grind" and was too frequently involved in "unnecessary arguments" with her peers and the instructors and should get some counseling.

Her first therapist was a man. "He was full of all kinds of advice about how a student, particularly a woman, shouldn't rock the boat. He kept telling me how to control myself and I got fed up with his paternalistic and authoritarian attitude," Joyce angrily commented. After she had been a social worker with her M.S.W. for three years, Joyce tried therapy again, this time with a woman. "I couldn't stand her weak, soft, supportive, namby-pamby attitude. So I quit. Each of the therapies lasted about five or six months."

Joyce eventually got to her reasons for seeing me. Again with much anger, she said, "I have never found a way to articulate my needs. I want to get ahead professionally and socially, but I do not have the necessary skills. Either I'm too aggressive and drive people away, or I'm too shy and never get myself heard." Joyce then went on to tell me that until now she had only had a few dates with men and "nothing has ever occurred." She confessed, "I've kissed one or two but that's about it."

Joyce and I arranged for her to come twice a week for her appointments. Because she was entirely self-supporting and with a modest income, I agreed to see her at a reduced fee.

Early Resistances

The ambivalence about coming into therapy with me that Joyce showed in her initial phone conversation re-emerged right after we agreed to work together. In the first interview after our consultation, she began by quoting the famous Rabbi Hillel, "If I am not for myself, who will be for me?" She then went on to inform me that all of her life she'd had to take care of herself; there was nobody on her side to support her or to nurture her. She elaborated on how distant her father had been, how narcissistic and infantile her mother had been, and how derogatory her brothers were of her. In addition, teachers, peers, relatives, virtually everybody "failed" her and made her "feel very mistrustful of the whole world."

Hearing Joyce's strong mistrust of "the whole world," I realized that she was also telling me that she had serious doubts about whether I would be for her. Therefore, I suggested, "Perhaps you are worried that I'll fail you too." Joyce's response showed her strong suspicions of me and intense anger toward me. "You get to the transference right away. You are quite narcissistic, aren't you?" she said with much indignation.

As I was silently studying my reactions to Joyce's hostile

outburst, realizing on one hand how vulnerable she must have been feeling, but also feeling irritated with her for her strong attack when I was trying to be helpful, I recognized how helpless I was experiencing myself to be. Joyce really did seem like the abusive, castrating seventh-grade schoolteacher from my past, and I inferred that I did not have much of a chance in modifying her attitude toward me.

While I was suffering in silence, Joyce once again rescued me by resuming her discourse. "There's no reason in the world for me to expect you to respect my strong identification with Judaism and my powerful affiliation with the women's movement." Recognizing her powerful wish for a fight with me and not wanting to appear too defensive lest I provoke her further, I answered, "I get the feeling you expect me to disrespect your identification with Judaism and to demean your affiliation with the women's movement."

Although Joyce continued to find fault with me and to try to argue with me, I sensed her anger was subsiding. However, she did go on to tell me that she knew I was a Freudian, a Jew, a male, and a social worker who had "come up through the ranks." Therefore, she concluded that I was "patrocentric, paternalistic, and patronizing." Though I might have given her supervisor the impression that I wasn't smug with women, she couldn't be sure.

One of the questions I began to pose to myself as I found myself to be the constant recipient of the slings and arrows of Joyce's outrageous fortune (and it was only the third week of treatment) was, "What is this woman doing with me? She keeps wondering about whether I can help her, seems to have lots of doubt about it; yet, she keeps coming to her appointments faithfully and doesn't talk about quitting." I began to hypothesize that Joyce might

actually like being with a man. However, she was behaving like a latency-age girl who likes boys but could
not admit this to herself. Therefore, to diminish her
anxiety she used the defense mechanism of reaction
formation and fought rather than let her libidinal wishes
emerge.

The more I thought about my hypothesis, the more it
began to appear like a real possibility. Joyce had not
renounced men. She was still eager to date them, but
when she got together with them, she drove them away
by arguing with them. Similarly, she was keeping her
"dates" with me, that is, her appointments, but had to
turn them into arguments. I also realized that the important men in her life, her father and her brothers, had given
her very little, and she resented them for this. Feeling put
down, weakened, and cut down by key men in her life,
she "identified with the aggressor" (A. Freud 1946) and
had to demean them.

As I became more objective about Joyce's plight and saw
her a little less as my castrating seventh-grade teacher and
more as a wounded woman who was fighting to preserve
her sanity, my empathy increased. Furthermore, I believe
my changing attitude became more visible to Joyce.

After about a month of sessions with the sparks continually flying in and around my office, Joyce brought in her
first dream. She was in a Hebrew school, one from her
childhood when she was about 9 years old, and in the
classroom she was having a temper tantrum. The teacher,
a man, was very calm and told her, "Let's figure out
what's hurting you so much because that's what gets you
very angry."

In analyzing her dream, Joyce commented, with a
mixture of sarcasm and joviality, "That dream is going to
make you too happy. Obviously I am your student and

you are trying to help me with my anger. Unconsciously I see you as somebody who is helpful. But I turn all the power over to you and that makes me very angry." I told Joyce that we could now better understand why it was difficult to trust me. If she gets my help, she feels small and weak and I appear big and strong. The discrepancy makes her feel as she did when she was a young girl vis-à-vis her father and brothers—angry and unequal.

Joyce was able to see that to make a man happy (as her dream would make me) was to surrender to him, to feel like "a slave" next to him, and to let him "gloat" while she suffered. Therefore, it was better to try to make the man suffer instead. This theme preoccupied us in our work for the next several months. Her major resistance was her power struggle with me and I had to deal, particularly early in the treatment, with some of my counterresistances that involved a power struggle with her.

Some Early Counterresistances

By the time Joyce Kaplansky became my patient, I had been very much influenced by the women's movement. Many of my colleagues, students, patients, friends, and relatives were instrumental in helping me face certain prejudices in myself and address some of my male chauvinistic fantasies and practices. As I confronted some of my fears, competition with, and envy of women, I liked myself more and did better therapeutic work, supervision, and teaching.

Inasmuch as Joyce was correct about my being a Freudian, a Jew, and a male who rose through the ranks in social work, I had to consider not only how much of an enemy

I appeared to Joyce but also whether some of Joyce's
perceptions about my biases toward women, particularly
Jewish women, had some validity. As I reflected on this
issue, I realized that just as I, in many ways, represented
"the hostile man" in Joyce's life, she represented "the
hostile woman" in my life. Not only was Joyce my angry
schoolteacher, but she also stirred up memories in me of
some power struggles with the women and girls in my
Jewish family and extended family.

Reflecting further on power struggles, I became aware
of a struggle I was having with women, Jewish and
non-Jewish, in the present. As my male confreres and I
were trying to address some of our biases and prejudices
toward women, I felt, from time to time, that our efforts
were depreciated by some of our women colleagues.
Occasionally, like Joyce, they appeared more interested in
fighting about differences than in reconciling them. Where
I thought this was particularly true was the way some
members of the women's movement demeaned Freud and
Freudian theory. Although Freud and psychoanalysis,
from its inception, brought many women into the profession and into leadership positions, to this day (Freeman
and Strean 1987), psychoanalysis has been mistreated and
distorted by some ardent feminists. A fairly typical hostile
attack may be seen in the following excerpt from *The
Psychology of Today's Woman* (Bernay and Cantor 1986):

> According to traditional psychoanalytic theory,
> women are seen as deviants from male norms with
> weak and compromised superegos; poor moral judg-
> ment; needy, dependent, and self-destructive person-
> alities, and aggressive and competitive masculine
> strivings. These assumptions lead to the interpretation
> of women's customary passive resolutions, as well as

their more contemporary assertive and achieving res-
olutions, as perversions. [p. 1]

Although Freud did not view the girl's superego development impartially, his bias has been corrected by many
contemporary analysts on many occasions (for example,
Fine 1979, Freeman and Strean 1987, Teitelbaum 1991).
Furthermore, when psychoanalysts are accused of
viewing normal aggressive acts of women as perversions,
it may be hypothesized that the women are protesting too
much.

My struggle with Joyce was in part my struggle with
those women colleagues who coped to some extent with
the unfair sexism they had experienced by being unfair to
psychoanalysis. Frequently in my work with Joyce I found
myself wanting to argue with her by correcting her.
Although I knew this would be horrible therapy, I would
occasionally fantasy myself saying to Joyce, "Joyce, look,
just because Freud believed that penis envy is a biological
fact of life, don't you realize that most writers today
believe that it is a cultural phenomenon imposed by
societal and familial folkways and mores?" When she
would quote a feminist attacking psychodynamic theory
and practice, in retaliation I would fantasy myself quoting
a psychoanalyst, such as from the following remarks of
Reuben Fine (1973):

> In view of the attack levied upon this concept [penis
> envy] by the Women's Liberation Movement, it
> should be emphasized that penis envy is essentially a
> clinical observation about what women feel, not a
> derogation of women. Psychoanalysis believes very
> strongly in the liberation of women, and should be

looked upon as one of the major movements in that
direction. [p. 13]

The more I permitted myself to fantasy arguments with
Joyce, the more I could appreciate my investment in
winning a battle. I had to face the fact that in certain ways
I was colluding with her to avoid the therapy. Slowly, I
began to see how very similar in many ways Joyce and I
were; both of us were "more human than otherwise"
(Sullivan 1953).

The other issue I had to face during the early phase of
treatment was that Joyce was not only an ardent feminist
but also an ardent Jew. For some of the time that I had
been seeing Jewish women in therapy, I had not recognized sufficiently the significance of their Jewishness
(Siegel and Cole 1991). All too often I assumed I knew
what a given Jewish symbol or ritual meant to my patient.
In working with Joyce, I continually had to remind myself
of what Melanie Kaye/Kantrowitz (1991) pointed out in
her paper "The Issue is Power: Some Notes on Jewish
Women and Therapy":

> Traditional therapy focuses on an individual explora-
> tion and healing; its very bias runs counter to the bias
> of Jewish culture, which is toward the collectivity. Not
> that the individual should be sacrificed to the commu-
> nity, but that the individual is profoundly connected
> to the community, so profoundly that separation is
> not truly possible without extreme loss. In some ways,
> this stance, deep in the Jewish tradition—as in the
> tradition of many oppressed peoples—corresponds to
> feminism. [p. 13]

It was very tempting at times to view Joyce's preoccupation with her "groups" as a resistance only, rather than

something that was also an expression of her ego ideals, her history, her libidinal wishes, and more. As I became more in tune with my own struggles with Joyce and feminism, I could better appreciate the saliency of collectivity in Joyce's psychic and real life.

Name Calling

One of the best ways for therapists to recognize that they are dealing with a negative countertransference is by noting how often they use diagnostic labels when thinking about or talking about their patients. Whenever I note in myself or in others a tendency to refer to a patient as "psychopathic," "sociopathic," "borderline," or "ambulatory schizophrenic," I begin to wonder about my own or my colleague's hostile feelings toward the patient. I have never heard a therapist say "I am very much enjoying my work with my psychopathic patient" or "I love that borderline patient." I have concluded, as have others (Erikson 1964, Fine 1982), that when a therapist is in a rejecting mood, unable to face his or her feelings of powerlessness, helplessness, and incompetency, the therapist can resort to diagnostic name calling. Instead of calling the patient "a son of a bitch," the therapist may use the term "psychopath."

Early in my work with Joyce, when I was particularly intimidated and angered by her attacks, I did use diagnostic labels as I thought about her. "Borderline" was one; "character disorder" was another. The use of these labels expressed my wish to counterattack and to avoid facing her feelings of vulnerability as well as my own.

As I found myself participating in a practice I had decried, I became aware of how similar diagnostic name calling is to other forms of name calling. In her paper

"Therapy's Double Dilemma: Anti-Semitism and Misogyny," Evelyn Torton Beck (1991) points out how anti-Semitism has combined with misogyny to create the stereotype of the "Jewish American Princess," frequently referred to as the "JAP." This name calling assaults the Jewish woman both as a woman and as a Jew.

Although I did not find myself referring to Joyce as a JAP, while working with her I thought of times I had used the label in thinking about other Jewish women patients. I concluded that diagnostic name calling is often a sophisticated form of baiting.

As I completed about three months of therapeutic work with Joyce, these were some of the counterresistance problems of which I became aware.

"It's Not a Man's World?"

As Joyce felt safer in facing her power struggles with men, helped in part, I believe, by her sensing unconsciously that I was undergoing a silent examination of my power struggle with her, she began to value her therapy much more. She arranged to increase the frequency of her sessions to four times a week, brought in more fantasies and dreams, examined important memories, and saw me much more as an ally.

During the next six months, Joyce's life changed dramatically. She became a supervisor at her agency, began to date men, wrote and published a professional article, and eventually became engaged to a man she "really respected," who "adored" her.

A fascinating dimension of this important and main phase of the treatment is that although Joyce completely resisted my invitation to free-associate on the couch, our examination of her reluctance to be on the couch helped her produce important material that was used very constructively in her therapy. At first, Joyce did not want to take the couch because she viewed being on it as undergoing a form of surgery whereby I would perform the equivalent of a lobectomy on her. In addition, she fantasied that I would extract blood from her, amputate parts of her, and eventually eradicate her completely.

As we examined Joyce's fantasies that I would annihilate her, we learned that during her childhood she had unconsciously viewed herself as a boy. However, she experienced her father's demeaning her as a castration and her brother's disrespect of her as amputations. Her vagina was not a part of her body that she could enjoy; it was a wound that appeared ugly and something to hide.

When Joyce could better understand why she had a distorted image of herself and faced the fact that she related to the world and to herself as if she were a castrated boy, she began to tone down her competition with men. In her fifth month of therapy, Joyce reflected, "I think I try to put men in the same position my father and brothers put me—weak, castrated, and devalued."

It was shortly after this insight that Joyce also began to reflect on her relationship with her mother. Masochistic, depressed, self-effacing, and a hypochondriac, Joyce's mother was a poor role model and did little to help Joyce enjoy being a woman.

As Joyce felt less competitive with me and less frightened of being destroyed by me, I thought she would be willing to use the couch. I was wrong. She felt that if she were on a couch and I was on a chair, it was "a terribly unequal" situation. I would feel superior to her as I gratified my sadistic and voyeuristic wishes while she suffered. "How about you taking the couch, Herb?" she suggested one day. When I asked Joyce how she would feel if I were on the couch and she were behind me, her response surprised me. "I would jump on top of you and rape the hell out of you!" Joyce retorted.

Although Joyce was becoming more sexually free with her fiancé, she tended to view a sexual union between a man and a woman as far from being a loving act. It was a sadomasochistic duel and part of a power struggle in which she was still very invested. Nonetheless, as Joyce fantasied raping me and me raping her, she became even more loving and libidinal with her fiancé. She also became more trusting of me, praising me on occasion for being "sensitive and empathetic."

As Joyce began to like herself more as a sexual woman and became more loving in many of her relationships — personal and professional — she began to see men more as they were and not just as hostile adversaries. "Women have a place in the world. It is not a man's world entirely," Joyce remarked with conviction in her eighth month of treatment.

Jewish Issues

Joyce's fiancé, Noah, although identified with Orthodox Judaism, was not as observant as Joyce. She became somewhat influenced by him and began to question her strict adherence to many Jewish rituals and practices.

Although premarital sexual relations are forbidden among the Orthodox, Joyce and Noah were having sex in the third month of their courtship. Joyce found herself attending synagogue services less, praying less, and occasionally eating meals in non-kosher restaurants.

In analyzing some of her reactions to moderating some of her religious practices, Joyce experienced herself initially as a defiant rebel. She had dreams of yelling and screaming at her father, saying she wasn't going to shul to hear his boring sermons; then she had her father yell back at her that she was a hypocrite. In another dream, she arranged for her father to recite the Kaddish (the mourner's prayer) because her "hypocrisy" made her a heathen, which in Jewish law was the same as being dead! Further analysis of this dream revealed that, in part, becoming less observant was experienced by Joyce as murdering her father, maiming God, and lashing out at the elders of the synagogue. For this, she deserved punishment.

As Joyce continually referred to Noah as "the nicest Jewish man I know," she concomitantly contrasted him with the Orthodox Jewish men with whom she was in contact most of her life. "They were smug, demeaning, and patronizing, and I think part of me unconsciously resented Judaism because it caters to men," Joyce lamented. She pointed out how the Torah, Talmud, and most Hebraic writing were male oriented. She expressed a great deal of rage about "men running the show and the shul."

One of the changes that Joyce made toward the end of her first year of treatment was changing her style of dress. She wore more modern clothes, stopped wearing the kerchief, and friends told her frequently that she was "looking sexy." While Joyce was beginning to enjoy her sexuality more, she had a dream in which she was mistaken for being gentile. Associations to the dream revealed that in her mind to be sexual was to be hostile toward Judaism. She began to feel like a religious convert.

Although Joyce took for granted that I was Jewish, she began to feel that I was the culprit who converted her to Christianity. In a dream she had at this time, she made me a Protestant minister who was baptizing her. After listening to Joyce go on for some time, feeling like she had been duped and turned into a Christian, I eventually was able to help her see that it was she who had written the script of her own dream. Therefore, the dream showed a disguised wish of hers to be a Christian.

At first, Joyce strenuously denied her wish to be a Christian and tried to engage me in arguments as if I were trying to convince her of something. However, when I maintained my neutrality, not only was Joyce able to acknowledge some fantasies of being "a sexy shiksa" [a sexy gentile woman], but she thought that if she were a Christian she would have more power and become a leader in the church. As we discussed this fantasy, Joyce was able to share with me a secret she had kept away from everyone most of her life. This was her wish to be a rabbi. Then she would be an equal of her father, brothers, "and all those guys who seem so high and mighty, including Herb Strean."

Joyce spent several sessions pointing out that it was "time enough" and that Orthodox Jews should ordain women as rabbis. She pointed out that Orthodoxy was the only branch of Judaism that did not ordain women "yet." Joyce bellowed, "Women have to learn the *halacha* [Jewish text and law] when we go to school. Though we know as much and can teach as well as men, they don't let us rise to the top." She decried the injustice and said, "I will never change my mind on this issue!"

A Hostile Transference Reemerges

When Joyce was pointing out that she would "never change" her mind about the unfairness of Orthodox

Jewish women not being ordained, I detected a similarity between the affect she showed and the affect she expressed in adamantly refusing to use the couch. It was as if she were suggesting that although she had made many changes, on certain issues she would not yield. Although this notion crossed my mind a few times, I thought it was not an uncommon attitude for someone who had been in therapy for only about one year.

As I was giving some thought to Joyce's rigidity, she surprised me one day by announcing, "I'm marrying Noah next month and will stop my therapy at the end of this month." Despite my remaining quiet, Joyce knew she had taken me by surprise, and probably sensed that she had punctured my professional narcissism. To myself I said, "Gee whiz! She has made so many gains and has derived so much from her therapy, why does she want to treat me this way?" I felt there was a dogmatic and uncaring attitude on Joyce's part as she announced her termination. I felt she was placing me in a position she had been in often—having to accept a situation without having a say in the matter. Perhaps it was like being shoved to the side at the synagogue where the women sit, or not being able to be ordained, or having to accept a weakened status and role as a girl in her own home. Furthermore, now that she had Noah, perhaps she had little use for me.

To test some of my hypotheses, I asked Joyce, "Could you tell me why you haven't wanted to discuss this decision with me?" At this, Joyce became furious and said indignantly, "Do I have to discuss everything with you? Do you have to be in on everything? You have to be the boss all of the time! I knew you would take your rigid Freudian stance on this. Look, I've recently told you how I wanted to be a rabbi, and while that may never be a possibility, when it comes to this therapy, I'm the one who is going to say 'Amen.' "

Not only had Joyce begun to feel again that her therapy was a manipulation on my part which was weakening her, but she also felt I made her undergo the equivalent of a religious conversion. "I am an Orthodox Jew and you are going to try to make me become an Orthodox Freudian!" she blurted out in intense anger. She was also convinced that I was trying to get her to study to be a psychoanalyst, which was "against [her] better principles."

Joyce also had another issue that bothered her, and which explained quite well her resistance to use the couch. "You know damn well you've wanted me to fall in love with you and want to have sex with you," she said accusingly. This was "a preposterous idea." "First of all, you are not my type. Second, you are not sexy and I like sex with a sexy man like Noah. Third, there's something not Jewish about you. You are *traif* [unkosher] and I want a clean man," Joyce uttered in a dismissing manner.

I tried to help Joyce examine more closely her strong negative transference, but despite my interpretations of her wish to turn me into a weak failure the way she was often treated, I was unable to convince Joyce to stay in treatment. Though she was able to acknowledge the many gains she made in her therapy, it was clear that sustaining the therapy would, in her mind, make me too strong and too happy. It would be like satisfying me sexually while she got little out of it. As I thought about her references to me as a lousy sexual partner, I couldn't help thinking that whatever limitations I had, staying in treatment with me would be for her the same as having forbidden incest with her father or brother.

I felt very disappointed that Joyce left treatment prematurely. I would have liked to continue to work with her so that we could have reduced some more of her hatred, helped her enjoy herself more as a sexual woman, and provided her with more self-esteem and self-confidence, which would have helped her experience men more realistically, rather than as so powerful next to her.

As I examined and reexamined my counterresistances, particularly my countertransference reactions to Joyce, I got in touch with an issue I had discussed many times in my personal analysis, namely, a residue of my relationship with my Jewish mother. My Jewish mother, like Joyce, was very critical of me, and I always tried to please her so that her criticisms would diminish, if not cease altogether. I was never very successful but kept trying. In hindsight, I can say that I related to Joyce with some of the same masochistic attitudes. I think Joyce unconsciously sensed this vulnerability in me and exploited it. Had I been more aware of this unconscious collusion, it may have made a difference in the way the treatment ended.

Yet, Joyce, like all patients, taught me a great deal about myself, the psychoanalytic process, psychodynamics, and human relationships. I became a more sensitive therapist as a result of working with her, particularly in my work with Orthodox Jewish women.

6

Summary
and
Conclusions

In the introduction to this book, I took note of the ambivalent attitude of dynamic psychotherapy toward religion and acknowledged that this attitude was matched by religion's ambivalence toward psychotherapy. I concurred with Leavy's (1993) comment: "The ignorance of psychoanalysts [and other therapists] on matters of religion is only equaled by the ignorance of psychoanalysis [and other therapies] on the part of the faithful" (p. 488).

Another preliminary recognition was that the difficulties psychotherapists have had in coping with and understanding religious behavior very much mirrored Freud's ambivalence toward his own religion, Judaism. Although Freud was an avowed atheist, he also was an active member of Jewish organizations, wrote frequently on Jewish subjects such as Jewish wit, Moses and monotheism, and the self-esteem and superego functioning of

Jews. Freud married an Orthodox Jewish woman and declared he would always remain a Jew (Jones 1953–1957, Meghnagi 1993).

In studying the psychotherapeutic literature from Freud's time to the present, I observed that religious themes have consistently tended to induce strong countertransference reactions in clinicians. Many therapists to this day still try to explain to their patients the irrational nature of religion, or at the opposite extreme, they have regarded religion as a private domain to be kept apart from psychotherapeutic investigation. At a recent panel discussion of a paper, "The Significance of Religious Themes During Psychoanalysis" (Grossman 1993), Jacob Arlow had to implore well-trained and experienced clinicians to treat religious experiences of their patients in the same neutral manner they respond to other clinical data and not attempt to validate or invalidate the religious orientation of their patients.

During the past two decades clinicians have had to examine their own biases toward religion much more carefully because some societal developments have influenced who their clientele are. The last two decades have brought to therapy many devout religious adherents who previously would have shunned it. Members of most religious groups, the devout included, are now leading more secular lives and are actively questioning, debating, and reevaluating traditional religious dogma and ritual. In her recent book *The History of God: The 4000-Year Quest of Judaism, Christianity, and Islam*, Karen Armstrong (1993) demonstrated that more and more people have found that the conventional religious customs no longer work for them. Consequently, they have been seeking guidance from experts outside the church or synagogue, and psychotherapy has been one institution to which they have turned.

Although many religious adherents are questioning some of the precepts of their faiths, another cultural development also has occurred. Many individuals who were psychotherapy patients but not religious adherents, though staying in therapy, are now affiliating themselves with religious institutions. For example, in a recent study, *A Generation of Seekers*, Wade Clark Roof (1993) concluded that the "outsized" generation born between 1946 and 1964 is now turning to religion. A group well known to therapists, they are the ones who were spiritually shaken by the 1960s, felt the aftershocks of the 1970s, and today only five percent of them declare themselves as either atheists (one percent) or agnostics.

As contemporary psychotherapists whose caseloads now contain many religious adherents, we are in a unique position to expose the unconscious meaning that religious behaviors and values have for their adherents. Psychotherapists can help answer the following questions. What kind of libidinal gratification do the religious practices provide? What defenses are at work and why? What are the differences and similarities between the superego mandates and ego ideals of the faithful, on one hand, and atheists and agnostics, on the other? Are there similarities and differences between their life histories, family relationships, and other object relations? Do different diagnostic groups that are part of the caseload of therapists exhibit different forms of religious behavior? By way of illustration, in a recent study by Meissner (1991) entitled "The Phenomenology of Religious Psychopathology," the author pointed out that psychotherapists should determine whether their patients' belief systems serve adaptive or neurotic purposes. He found that hysterical patients seem drawn to religious systems that foster intense emotional experience and irrational belief. Obsessional and depressed patients tend to seek perfectionism in their religious practices. Depressed patients tend to express their incapacity to achieve perfection and believe in their inherent sinfulness; they seem to feel condemned. Narcissistic patients, in addition to sharing pathological traits similar to those shown by depressed and obsessional patients, often exhibit attitudes of religious superiority. Patients can also translate masochistic attitudes into religious practices. These are prominent in Christians who identify themselves with the suffering Christ in the hope that this will be the path to divine love. Paranoid patients tend to be authoritarian in their outlook, focusing on power. This attracts them to strong leaders and inspires hostility toward those who have different belief systems.

To answer some of the questions posed above, I decided to study one branch of Judaism, Orthodox Judaism. Many Orthodox Jews have been seeking out therapists, particularly during the last decade and a half, so that their numbers were sufficient to permit some intensive case studies.

This study was conducted in New York City, where fourteen percent of Jews identify themselves as Orthodox, compared with seven percent nationwide (Goldman 1993). Four cases of Orthodox Jews seen in psychoanalytic psychothererapy were selected for intensive examination. Although the number of subjects is very small and the study sample of two men and two women may not be representative, the dynamics of the patients studied, particularly as expressed in their religious behavior and responses to treatment, offer rich clinical data on Orthodox Jews that has not been presented heretofore. I also thought this project would be particularly invigorated by a case study of individuals, who for many years shunned psychotherapy, viewing it as something sacrilegious.

Before reporting on the part of this study that involved sitting in on the psychotherapy sessions of four Orthodox Jews, I shall summarize some of the psychodynamic hypotheses that evolved from my review of the major beliefs and rituals of Orthodox Jews prior to my meeting the patients under study.

One of the initial difficulties was in trying to define Orthodox Judaism. Although I did not come up with a definitive answer, Judaism, like all religions, can be viewed as a faith, an identity, a hope, and an over-whelming passion (Fromm 1950, Kahn 1968, Wolpe 1990). Again, similar to most religions, Judaism involves the worship of a God who is supernatural, omnipotent, omniscient, and deserving of unambivalent obedience.

Orthodox Jews can be described as those Jews who accept the fullness of Jewish law and tradition (Kahn 1968). They view the Torah as divine revelation, a direct creation of God's hand. It is to be obeyed and believed without question. The Orthodox are the most disciplined of Jews and they stand for positive old values. They live a life replete with prayers, seeking out God three to eight times a day. They have a constant, deep, and private understanding with their God and never question His existence. Orthodox Judaism is a more demanding way of life than that of most other branches of Judaism (Reform, Reconstructionist, and Conservative), and the Orthodox Jew is continually immersed in ritual and prayer from dawn to dusk.

Because God is so central to Orthodox Judaism, I have spent a good portion of this exploration in trying to understand what God means to the Orthodox Jew. Ac-

cording to the scriptures, He made the world, and each of
His acts was and is for the benefit of human beings. The
Jewish God is dependent upon human beings to influence
the world inasmuch as humanity and God participate as
partners.

The Bible tells us that God is like a lonely parent,
yearning for his children's love. The God of the "Children
of Israel" is a jealous god who frequently commands "You
shall have no other gods before me." God has many
feelings. He weeps, smiles, can be angry and fickle.
Because of a strong desire to nurture, God is both an
omnipotent mother and father. However, God is also a
rather narcissistic parental figure. Throughout the Bible
we note that He is more especially the friend of those who
care for Him.

Similar to children who imitate and identify with their
parents, Orthodox Jews imitate and identify with their
God. To be godlike, Orthodox Jews aspire to be eternally
compassionate and consistently loving.

Despite God's omnipotence and omniscience, He does
not arrange for the world to be perfect. Hence, Orthodox
Jews practice their faith in anger, arguing with God and
wondering why He has not been more beneficent. Although angry at Him for not granting permanent peace on
earth, the Orthodox have a tendency to turn their anger
against themselves and become more devout, obedient,
and masochistic.

Because God is so much the ever-present parent in the
Orthodox Jew's life, real parent–child relationships,
though important, occupy less concern in the Bible and
elsewhere. The synagogue is referred to as the House of
God, and many an Orthodox Jew spends more time in
God's home than in his or her own.

Orthodox Jews very much believe they are God's

Chosen People, and for God's favor they owe Him complete obedience. Although they are completely devoted to God, Orthodox Jews cannot fully or even partially understand His motives or behavior.

After reviewing what the Hebrew sages have said about God and observing how Orthodox Jews relate to Him, I paused to consider how God is experienced by the Orthodox from a psychodynamic perspective. From this perspective, God is a fantasy, an imaginary notion, because He or She cannot be observed nor accounted for in any scientific sense. In psychoanalysis all phenomena have causes, and no one has been able to demonstrate who He is and how God was created. Therefore, to talk to someone or something that cannot be reached by sensing, hearing, or with some other sense is, according to psychoanalytic theory, acting out an illusion (Freud 1927).

Just as a child who feels helpless in the absence of a parent or parental surrogate can hallucinate a parent and then feel a diminution of anxiety, the Orthodox Jew hallucinates a Father in heaven and feels less anxiety. Also, when a child cannot rely on parents to provide the kind of life he or she yearns for, an omnipotent and omniscient parent is fantasied. God is the omnipotent and omniscient parent for the Orthodox. From a psychodynamic point of view, the more helplessness and desperation a human being experiences, the more he or she needs a protective figure. The powerful need for an everpresent God among Orthodox Jews suggests that without their God, they would feel boundless terror—the kind of terror Jews have felt throughout their history.

Orthodox Jews never need to be reminded of the long history of Jewish persecution, highlighted by events ranging from the twelfth-century pogrom in York, England, which led to the banishment of Jews from that country, to the Spanish Inquisition of the fifteenth century, to the pogroms of Russia in the early years of this century. Those who lived in the 1930s and 1940s will never forget the Second World War when Hitler's rise to power in Germany led to the destruction of a thriving and apparently well-assimilated German Jewish community (Sklare 1960). To Orthodox Jews, steeped in these stories, the existence of a God who works in ways no one can fully fathom is quite plausible.

In studying the Orthodox Jew's very subordinate, submissive, obedient relationship to God, I was able to better understand common character traits of Orthodox Jews — arrogance and masochism. When faithful Jews are required to be subordinate to an all-powerful God, they begin to resent their weakened position. Like children who resent their parents' power and compete with their parents to wrest it away, Orthodox Jews compete with God and often appear dogmatic and authoritarian. Yet, when children compete with and resent their parents, they cannot do so indefinitely because they want their parents' love and protection. Orthodox Jews go back and forth like ambivalent children, submitting to God, resenting doing so, then competing with God, feeling guilty and anxious about it, and then returning once again to a submissive position with Him.

I came to view the struggle that the Orthodox Jewish man has with God as very similar, if not identical, to an acute oedipal struggle. He resents God's power and dominion, fights with God for it, becomes panicky about fighting with the One he idealizes, and then submits to God, taking a negative oedipal, or latent homosexual, position with Him. My experiences suggested the inference that the Orthodox Jewish man who frequently feels like a masochistic woman next to God must build defenses to denounce, repress, and suppress his effeminate position next to God. One way to do this is to thank God every morning for one's not being a woman. Another way is to segregate women in the synagogue and elsewhere and make sure women have an inferior position to men that pervades all interpersonal relationships. The Orthodox Jewish woman is placed next to her male counterpart as the Orthodox Jewish man is next to God—subordinated, demeaned, weakened, and angry. As a result, both Orthodox Jewish men and women who are often angry and guilty individuals cannot enjoy each other in a sustained, loving way.

My experience suggests that many of the compulsive rituals that preoccupy Orthodox Jews are a means of warding off id wishes to destroy, regress, and become polymorphous perverse.

Being restricted in many ways, having to endure much frustration in every area of living, the Orthodox Jew develops strong fantasies to rebel. Because rebellion against God and the faith is such a severe crime in his or her mind, the Orthodox Jew needs to develop and maintain a powerful superego. Instead of libidinal and aggressive gratification, Orthodox Jews submit to their powerful superegos and constantly champion justice, mercy, mutual aid, and humility. The prophets who are frequently quoted by Orthodox Jews are forever preaching moral perfection. Moral perfection, which is close to a command that is obeyed daily by Orthodox Jews, helps them defend against strong wishes to be imperfect. Reaction formation is one of the favorite defenses of the Orthodox Jew. Feeling very guilty about his or her strong wishes to rebel and regress gives rise in the Orthodox Jew to "unusually stringent ethical ideals" (Freud 1939, p. 134).

I have noted repeatedly that Judaism has a highly

intellectual tradition where reason and rigorous thought have a central place (Wolpe 1990). Readiness to undergo all manner of privation in the pursuit of learning has always been a characteristic of Orthodox Jewish life. To read and to study for the Orthodox Jew is to be loved by an omnipotent and omniscient God. Reading, researching, and studying is, in his or her unconscious, having a mutually loving, adoring, and rewarding conversation with a beloved parent.

As Orthodox Jews acquire more and more knowledge, they assign themselves an elite status. Orthodox Jews have a self-confidence and a narcissism that helps them value themselves and enjoy success.

All of these issues emerged in the case studies of the four individuals discussed above. Let me now summarize what I observed from my meetings with them.

The Case Studies

As I have reiterated, four Orthodox Jews from New York City who seek out the same therapist hardly constitute a representative sample of Orthodox Jews in psychotherapy. Nonetheless, to reflect on what they share regarding their presenting problems, family backgrounds, internal dynamics, views on Judaism, and responses to the treatment situation may shed some light on the questions posed at the onset of this book. It is my hope that these case studies may stimulate other psychotherapists to undertake similar ventures.

Presenting Problems

All four members of the sample initiated psychotherapy themselves or readily accepted referral. In contrast to

many individuals who enter a therapist's consultation
room because they are pressured or mandated to have
therapy, David, Rachel, Meyer, and Joyce recognized that
they had problems of their own making and were ready to
take much of the responsibility to resolve their internal
conflicts. All members of the sample, therefore, were well
motivated for treatment, did not project their difficulties
onto others to any appreciable extent, and were willing to
face themselves in front of another person toward whom
they showed some basic trust. What most demonstrated
was a good prognosis for treatment (Fine 1982). Furthermore, all of the subjects continued to attend their sessions
faithfully and increased the frequency of their sessions
after being in treatment for a year or less. Three out of four
of the patients continued in their intensive treatment until
a mutual termination date was set. All of this suggests that
the Orthodox Jewish patient is an exceptionally good
candidate for psychotherapy.

Regarding the specific problems that they presented at
their initial interviews, all four patients were upset about
facets of their interpersonal relationships. David and Rachel were distressed about their relationships with their
respective spouses, and Meyer and Joyce wanted treatment in order to better their interpersonal relationships,
particularly with the opposite sex. We can infer from this
observation that the Orthodox Jew is object oriented,
wants to increase his or her capacity to love and to reduce
hatred, and sees himself or herself as a major instrument
in accomplishing this objective.

All four of my patients had serious sexual problems.
David and Meyer had potency problems, and Rachel and
Joyce suffered frequently from lack of sexual desire. All of
the subjects suffered from conflicts involving their sexual
identities. The men struggled to avoid facing their envy of

women, and the women struggled with, but were more conscious than the men of, their envy of their male counterparts. From this sample I can reaffirm what I hypothesized at the beginning of this volume, namely, that the Orthodox Jew suffers from sexual problems and is quite shaky about his or her gender identity (though of course this is not unique to Orthodox Jews).

Masochism and depression were also very visible in all of the subjects. The Orthodox Jew, although harboring a great deal of sadism, tends to turn it inward and suffers from much self-hatred. The suffering the Orthodox Jew experiences shows itself in low self-esteem, depression, and poor body image. In addition, the subjects manifested psychosomatic problems from time to time.

Family Backgrounds

Three of the four patients under examination came from Orthodox Jewish homes where their parents were very observant. Meyer was the exception. In all four cases the father was described by the patient as a strict disciplinarian, harsh, authoritarian, and punitive. He was further experienced as very narcissistic, with little spontaneous warmth shown toward his children. Usually he was preoccupied with religious rituals and synagogue commitments.

The mothers of the subjects were almost universally described as self-effacing, masochistic, deferential to their husbands, occasionally hypochondriacal, and usually quite depressed. Mothers usually supported fathers in maintaining strict discipline. Physical punishment was not unknown in the households.

Our two women patients clearly resented their brothers inasmuch as the status of the male child was a higher one in the home. In none of the families under study could it be said that there were warm sibling relationships that impacted positively on our patients.

Achievement was an important issue in at least three of the four families. The Orthodox Jew is one who is told to get ahead and is often pressured to do so. Usually he or she wants to comply but may secretly rebel.

In three of the four cases, the patients spent a great deal of their waking hours as a child, teenager, and into adulthood in the synagogue. The shul was in many ways more of a home than were their own residences. God was certainly a more important parental figure than either their mothers or fathers. The congregants of the synagogue were as central in their lives as were family members, if not more so.

All of the patients came from homes that were economically secure. Though making money was important, it was not overemphasized.

Dynamics

After reviewing these patients' presenting problems and family backgrounds, the internal dynamics they share are reasonably clear. Basic to the internal functioning of the Orthodox Jew is a strong pressure to conform—to religious edicts, to parental mandates, to community obligations, and more. As the Orthodox Jewish child feels obligated to conform to many commands, in addition to the ten commandments, he or she becomes very resentful. The resentment is usually contained, turned against the self, and a punitive superego evolves.

The punitive superego can account for the masochism, self-hatred, depression, and poor self-esteem noted in all of our subjects. Because Jewish girls are demeaned and derogated at home and in the synagogue, they hate boys and men. Although they resent their submissive roles and suffer from much penis envy, they keep their sadism to themselves and hate themselves. This was particularly clear in the case of Rachel, but despite Joyce's more open fight, she nonetheless suffered from low self-esteem. For the women patients, their mothers were poor role models and as a result, happiness for themselves as women had to be found; it did not seem too available.

The women patients submitted to the men in the same way David and Meyer submitted to God and the synagogue elders. The men, like the women, did not like themselves very much and were too guilty to enjoy much pleasure. As mentioned, they had to work overtime to deny their envy of the women's seemingly less burdensome life. Latent but strong homosexuality existed in all our subjects.

Despite the Orthodox Jew's severe superego with its attendant problems in sexual functioning, self-esteem, and gender identity, the disciplined life he or she has endured tends to assist in the formation of some strong ego functions. The judgment, impulse control, and frustration tolerance of all our subjects, with the possible exception of Meyer, were in good shape. Object relations were also working reasonably well for most of the subjects. That part of the superego known as the ego ideal provided many positive, affirmative mandates such as kindness, charity, and love, which placated the severe superego and provided a boost to the patients' self-image. Through these virtues the patients never felt alone.

Because conflicts on the phallic-oedipal level were severe, all of our patients regressed and immersed themselves in many rituals. The rituals were a means of coping with the ambivalence toward their parental introjects, whom they resented but needed. All of our subjects, to a degree more marked than in most patients, struggled between a wish to comply and a wish to disobey all authorities. Although they were all active, assertive individuals, they feared their own aggression and the aggression of others. Pleasure was experienced as "too gratifying" and "too rebellious." Hence, self-punishment was seen frequently in all of our subjects, particularly after gratifying id wishes.

All of our subjects were intellectually curious and essentially conflict-free in the areas of learning and working. Bright, energetic, vigorous, and loving in many ways, our subjects all suffered from low self-esteem, fear of aggression, problems in gender identity, sexual anxiety, and depression. Despite their strong ego functions, their severe and punitive superegos interfered with consistently enjoyable psychosexual functioning.

Views on Judaism

None of the patients in my sample entered treatment with any conscious conflict with God, but after they had been in treatment about a year, all four of them revealed strong feelings of resentment toward Him. In effect, our patients showed a strong disillusionment with their Father in Heaven for not being as omnipotent and omniscient as they initially thought Him to be. Further, when our patients could genuinely accept their rage toward God, it was a painful experience for all of them. Initially they felt manipulated by the therapist for "converting" them to a new religion. When this attitude was difficult for them to contain, they became very lonely and somwhat desperate. Facing their desperation and loneliness, and relating it to the stories of their lives, all of our subjects made peace with their God. They did not disavow Him but became less preoccupied with Him and less intimidated by Him.

The patients shifted their positions with God much as most patients in dynamic psychotherapy shift their positions toward parental introjects. Often, after facing certain hatreds, the modal patient feels lost and lonely. If he or she can weather the storm, ego functions get stronger, and parental introjects become less intimidating and hated. Inasmuch as Orthodox Jews cathect God as an object more than they do in regard to their own parents, we should expect shifts in feelings toward God in their therapy and use these shifts as a barometer of psychic change.

It should be noted, however, that the Orthodox Jewish patient's transference toward God is very much influenced by the relationship he or she has with his or her parents. Just as all of the patients experienced their fathers as authoritarian, punitive, and narcissistic, God was experienced similarly. And just as these patients felt deprived of emotional nurturance from their mothers, God was experienced frequently as emotionally nonsupportive.

Few clinicians would view a continued hating of parents as successful treatment. So I tentatively suggest that for the Orthodox Jew, a noncombative acceptance of God may be regarded as a successful outcome of treatment. This was observed in almost all of the subjects.

All of these subjects during the course of therapy voiced a great deal of resentment toward the Orthodox Jewish lifestyle, sometimes expressed in wishing to be Christian. The pressure to undertake various rituals such as constant praying, synagogue attendance, and periodic sexual abstinence was something that infuriated them, but they felt helpless to do anything to modify the pressure they were under. However, as they resolved hatreds toward God, parental introjects, and the therapist, they felt less pressure to conform to a rigid adherence to rituals. Thus, rituals may be viewed psychodynamically as parental injunctions the Orthodox Jew feels compelled to obey. When he or she feels less intimidated by internalized authority, performing rituals seems less obligatory.

Much of a rigid Orthodox Jewish way of life seems related to a punitive and severe superego. As a result of being in therapy, when God and parental introjects come to be viewed by the Orthodox Jew as not so high and mighty, there is less hatred of them. Feeling less intimidated by introjects, the Orthodox Jew becomes more emotionally spontaneous and less fearful of punishment. Decisions about how to live become more influenced by reality considerations than by inner commands.

In undergoing therapy, Orthodox Jews, like most individuals who participate in it, become more loving yet more autonomous, less rebellious but more independent, less narcissistic but more object related. As a result, they can enjoy their God more but need Him less, participate in the synagogue and in other Jewish settings with more pleasure and less fear, pray and obey rituals selectively, with more satisfaction.

Course of Treatment

With the exception of Joyce's termination phase, all four of the patients I have discussed coped with their therapy and the therapist quite similarly. All of them initiated or readily accepted referral to treatment. All of them were ready to explore their inner lives and take responsibility for their difficulties. Yet, all of the patients initially resisted the therapeutic process, viewing the therapist as a dogmatic, authoritarian person. In their minds he did not appear too different from their authoritarian fathers or their narcissistic God.

When each of the patients recognized that the therapist would not censure them nor retaliate when opposed, all welcomed his neutral position. From a resistive position they all moved into a positive transference and enjoyed "a honeymoon" (Fine 1982) with the therapist.

It would appear that Orthodox Jews who have been subjected to many rigid dogmas, and to real and imagined authoritarian personalities, particularly welcome an unconditional positive response from the therapist. Like a rescued child, they "fall in love" with the therapist, increase the frequency of their sessions, and begin to seriously examine their lives. In contrast to their own punitive superegos, the therapist appears to be a very benign superego. Consequently, they feel less guilty, more likable, and become more loving. The noncritical, accepting posture of the therapist to the Orthodox Jew is experienced as a unique gift.

As the patients accepted themselves more, felt better understood by a parental figure than hitherto, and feared their own aggression much less, they began to examine more intensively their ties and involvement with Orthodox Judaism. As already reported, they eventually became disillusioned with an omnipotent God and questioned their rigid adherence to rituals. At this time, all of the subjects became wary of the therapist, who was experienced as another God who failed them. Rather than question their loyalty to Judaism, they tried to fight it out with the therapist. When they did not find the therapist joining them in battle, they began, like struggling, ambivalent adolescents, to accept and reject what seemed appropriate in Judaism, in psychotherapy, and in life. This "working through" phase was tedious for the patients but yielded positive results.

It would appear that dynamically oriented psychotherapy is eminently suited for Orthodox Jews, and that Orthodox Jews are individuals with whom dynamically oriented therapists can do some of their best work. Because they are usually well motivated for treatment, Orthodox Jews will be welcomed by therapists who naturally enjoy working with well-motivated patients. The Orthodox Jew is usually object related, introspective, and has the kind of guilt within that makes him or her a very responsible individual in the treatment situation. These qualities usually induce a very positive response in many therapists.

The Orthodox Jew usually likes to learn, and most therapists like to teach. This is a great boon to the therapeutic alliance that can easily evolve between the Orthodox Jewish patient and the therapist.

For patients to grow in psychotherapy requires of them discipline, frustration tolerance, trust, and an eagerness to learn about the self. The Orthodox Jew frequently brings these capacities to the treatment situation and the therapist frequently welcomes them. In sum, the Orthodox Jew and the dynamically oriented therapist can rather easily form a complementary relationship whereby much growth occurs in the patient.

One of the major findings of this study, if not *the* major finding, is that if the therapist approaches religious behavior and religious fantasies in the same way that all behavior is examined—dynamically, genetically, structurally, topographically—the Orthodox Jewish patient becomes a more loving and constructive human being who does not repudiate his or her religion but practices it more maturely and with more pleasure and flexibility. This assumes, of course, that the therapist is aware of and can monitor his or her positive and negative feelings and attitudes toward Orthodox Jews and Orthodox Judaism.

As Ostow (1982), Meghnagi (1993), and others (for example, Bergmann 1982) have noted, adherents of Orthodox Judaism and of dynamic psychotherapy have much in common. Both are societally marginal groups who have been demeaned, derogated, and have experienced much hostile discrimination toward themselves. Both emphasize the value of learning and the premise that knowledge is acquired when there is a positive alliance between teacher and learner. Both have to contend with opposition from within their own large group. Orthodox Jews have to coexist with Reform and Conservative Jews, and psychotherapy has within it many factions, dynamically oriented psychotherapy being only one of them.

Because dynamically oriented psychotherapy and Orthodox Judaism both teach that maturity and "the good life" can be obtained through knowledge of the self, they will probably continue to enjoy each other, learn from each other, and learn to respect and better understand differences between them that will always exist.

References

Arlow, J. (1951a). The consecration of the prophet. *Psychoanalytic Quarterly* 23:374–397.

_____ (1951b). A psychoanalytic study of a religious rite: Bar Mitzvah. *Psychoanalytic Quarterly* 6:353–374.

_____ (1979). Metaphor in the psychoanalytic situation. *Psychoanalytic Quarterly* 48:363–385.

Armstrong, K. (1993). *The History of God: The 4000 Year Quest of Judaism, Christianity and Islam*. New York: Knopf.

Beck, E. (1991). Therapy's double dilemma: Anti-semitism and misogyny. In *Seen But Not Heard: Jewish Women in Therapy*, ed. R. Siegel and E. Cole, pp. 19–30. New York: Harrington Park.

Bergler, E. (1969). *Selected Papers of Edmund Bergler*. New York: Grune & Stratton.

Bergmann, M. (1982). Moses and the evolution of Freud's Jewish identity. In *Judaism and Psychoanalysis*, ed. M. Ostow, pp. 111–142. New York: Ktav.

_____ (1992). *In the Shadow of Moloch: The Sacrifice of Children and its Impact on Western Religions.* New York: Columbia University Press.

Bernay, T., and Cantor, D. (1986). *The Psychology of Today's Woman.* Hillsdale, NJ: Analytic Press.

Birnbaum, P. (1964). *A Book of Jewish Concepts.* New York: Hebrew Publishing Company.

Brenner, C. (1955). *An Elementary Textbook of Psychoanalysis.* New York: International Universities Press.

Carter, S. (1993). *The Culture of Disbelief.* New York: Basic Books.

Erikson, E. (1950). *Childhood and Society.* New York: Norton.

_____ (1964). *Insight and Responsibility.* New York: Norton.

Fenichel, O. (1945). *Psychoanalytic Theory of Neuroses.* New York: Norton.

Ferenczi, S. (1955). *The Problems and Methods of Psychoanalysis,* vol. 3. New York: Basic Books.

Fine, R. (1973). Psychoanalysis. In *Current Psychotherapies,* ed. R. Corsini, pp. 1–34. Itasca, IL: F. E. Peacock.

_____ (1979). *The History of Psychoanalysis.* New York: Columbia University Press.

_____ (1982). *The Healing of the Mind.* New York: Free Press.

Freeman, L., and Strean, H. (1987). *Freud and Women.* New York: Continuum.

Freud, A. (1946). *The Ego and the Mechanisms of Defense.* New York: International Universities Press.

Freud, S. (1900). The interpretation of dreams. *Standard Edition* 4: 1–623.

_____ (1905a). Jokes and their relation to the unconscious. *Standard Edition* 8:3–247.

_____ (1905b). Three essays on the theory of sexuality. *Standard Edition* 7:125–230.

_____ (1912). The dynamics of transference. *Standard Edition* 12:97–108.

_____ (1914). On narcissism. *Standard Edition* 12:67–104.

_____ (1921). Group psychology and the analysis of the ego. *Standard Edition* 18:67–143.

_____ (1923). The ego and the id. *Standard Edition* 19:3–66.

_____ (1927). The future of an illusion. *Standard Edition* 21:5–56.

_____ (1930). Civilization and its discontents. *Standard Edition* 21:57–145.

_____ (1939). Moses and monotheism. *Standard Edition* 23:7–137.

Fromm, E. (1950). *Psychoanalysis and Religion*. New Haven: Yale University Press.

Glover, E. (1955). *The Technique of Psychoanalysis*. New York: International Universities Press.

Goldman, A. (1993). Religion notes. *The New York Times*, October 23, 1993, p. 12.

Greenson, R. (1967). *The Technique of Psychoanalysis*, vol. 1. New York: International Universities Press.

_____ (1992). The conflict between psychoanalysis and religion. In *On Loving, Hating, and Living Well: The Public Psychoanalytic Lectures of Ralph Greenson*, ed. R. Nemiroff, A. Sugarman, and A. Robins, pp. 41–56. New York: International Universities Press.

Grossman, L. (1993). The significance of religious themes and fantasies during psychoanalysis. *Journal of the American Psychoanalytic Association* 45:755–764.

Hartmann, H. (1964). *Essays on Ego Psychology*. New York: International Universities Press.

Heschel, S. (1991). Jewish feminism and women's identity. In *Seen but Not Heard: Jewish Women in Therapy*, ed. R. Siegel and E. Cole, pp. 31–40. New York: Harrington Park.

Jones, E. (1953–1957). *Sigmund Freud: Life and Work*, vols. 1–3. London: Hogarth.

Kahn, R. (1968). *The Passionate People*. New York: Fawcett World Library.

Kaye/Kantrowitz, M. (1991). The issue is power: Some notes on Jewish women and therapy. In *Seen but Not Heard: Jewish Women in Therapy*, ed. R. Siegel and E. Cole, pp. 7–18. New York: Harrington Park.

Kernberg, O. (1976). *Object Relations Theory and Clinical Psychoanalysis*. New York: Jason Aronson.

Klein, M. (1957). *Envy and Gratitude*. New York: Basic Books.

Kushner, H. (1993). *To Life: A Celebration of Jewish Being and Thinking*. Boston: Little, Brown.

Leavy, S. (1993). Book review of *Religion in Psychodynamic Perspective: The Contributions of Paul W. Pruyser. The Psychoanalytic Quarterly* 62(3):486–488.

Mahler, M. (1968). *On Human Symbiosis and the Vicissitudes of Individuation*. New York: International Universities Press.

Malony, H. N., and Spilka, B. (1991). *Religion in Psychodynamic Perspective: The Contributions of Paul W. Pruyser*. New York: Oxford University Press.

Meghnagi, D. (1993). *Freud and Judaism*. London: Karnac Books.

Meissner, W. (1991). The phenomenology of religious psychopathology. *Bulletin of the Menninger Clinic* 40:281–298.

Neumann, E. (1955). *The Great Mother*. New York: Pantheon.

Nemiroff, R., Sugarman, A., and Robins, A. (1992). *On Loving, Hating, and Living Well: The Public Psychoanalytic Lectures of Ralph Greenson*. New York: International Universities Press.

Nunberg, H. (1955). *Principles of Psychoanalysis*. New York: International Universities Press.

Ostow, M. (1982). Judaism and psychoanalysis. In *Judaism and Psychoanalysis*, ed. M. Ostow. New York: Ktav.

—— (1982). The Jewish response to crisis. In *Judaism and Psychoanalysis*, ed. M. Ostow, pp. 231–266. New York: Ktav.

Polsky, H. (1960). A study of orthodoxy in Milwaukee. In *The Jews*, ed. M. Sklare. Glencoe, IL: Free Press.

Prager, D., and Telushkin, J. (1981). *Nine Questions People Ask about Judaism*. New York: Simon & Schuster.

Reik, T. (1931). *Ritual: Psychoanalytic Studies*. New York: Farrar, Straus.

—— (1941). *Masochism in Modern Man*. New York: Grove.

—— (1951). *Dogma and Compulsion: Psychoanalytic Studies of Religion and Myths*. New York: International Universities Press.

—— (1959). *Mystery on the Mountain*. New York: Harper and Brothers.

Roof, W. C. (1993). *A Generation of Seekers*. New York: HarperCollins.

Rosen, B. (1960). Minority group in transition: A study of adolescent religious conviction and conduct. In *The Jews: Social Patterns of An American Group*, ed. M. Sklare, pp. 336–346. Glencoe, IL: Free Press.

Rubenstein, R. (1982). The meaning of anxiety in rabbinic Judaism. In *Judaism and Psychoanalysis*, ed. M. Ostow, pp. 73–110. New York: Ktav.

Siegel, R., and Cole, E., eds. (1991). *Seen but Not Heard: Jewish Women in Therapy*. New York: Harrington Park.

Sklare, M. (1960). *The Jews*. Glencoe, IL: Free Press.

Smith, J., and Handelman, S. (1990). *Psychoanalysis and Religion*. Baltimore: Johns Hopkins University Press.

Strean, H. (1985a). *Resolving Marital Conflicts*. New York: John Wiley and Sons.

_____ (1985b). The psychoanalyst: An agent of social change. *Current Issues in Psychoanalytic Practice* 2:29–37.

_____ (1990). *Resolving Resistances in Psychotherapy*. New York: Brunner/Mazel.

_____ (1993a). *Resolving Counterresistances in Psychotherapy*. New York: Brunner/Mazel.

_____ (1993b). *Jokes: Their Purpose and Meaning*. Northvale, NJ: Jason Aronson.

Strean, H., and Freeman, L. (1991). *Our Wish to Kill: The Murder in All Our Hearts*. New York: St. Martin's.

Sullivan, H. S. (1953). *The Interpersonal Theory of Psychiatry*. New York: Norton.

Teitelbaum, S. (1991). Countertransference and its potential for abuse. *Clinical Social Work* 19:267–277.

The Torah. (1962). Philadelphia: Jewish Publication Society of America.

Wolpe, D. (1990). *The Healer of Shattered Hearts*. New York: Henry Holt.

Index

Ego, religion and, xiv
Elitism, Orthodox Judaism and, 37–38
Erikson, E., 83, 135
Erotic transference, masochism case, 81

Family
backgrounds of, Orthodox Judaism, 158–159
dynamics of, Orthodox Judaism, 159–161
Father–child relationship. *See also* Mother–child relationship
aggression and, 56
ambivalence case, 56–57, 59–61, 63
born-again case, 104, 116, 117
dream analysis and, 51–52
feminist case, 126–127, 137
masochism case, 73, 78–79, 80, 81
Orthodox Judaism, 158–161
transference and, 66
Feminist case, 123–143
ambivalence, 124–125
couch, 137–138
counterresistances, 131–136
hostile transference, 140–143
initial session, 125–128
Jewish issues, 138–140
referral, 123
resistance (early sessions), 128–131
Fenichel, O., 106
Ferenczi, S., 32
Fine, R., 50, 52, 54, 133–134, 135, 157, 164
Free association
ambivalence case, 55
masochism case, 81
Freeman, L., 58, 133
Freud, A., 45, 63, 67, 78, 103, 130
Freud, S., xiii, xiv, xv, 4, 6, 15,
18, 19, 22, 32, 33, 34, 38, 63, 83, 91, 117, 133, 147–148, 153, 155
Fromm, E., 3, 4, 7, 151
Fromm-Reichman, F., 67

Gender problems, Orthodox Judaism, 18–20
Glover, E., 58
God
attitudes toward, of patients, 161–163
Orthodox Judaism and, 9–13, 151–152
parent–child relationship and, 152–154
sex role and, 89–90
transference and, 52–53, 162–163
Goldman, A., 150
Greenson, R., xiii, 8, 16, 18, 104
Grossman, L., xiv, xvi, 6, 148

Handelman, S., xv, 6
Hartmann, H., 37
Homosexuality. *See also* Gender problems
latent
ambivalence case, 59–61
Orthodox Judaism and, 154–155
transference, born-again case, 114
Honeymoon phase
ambivalence case, 52–55
masochism case and, 78–80
Hysteria, religion and, 150

Incest, ambivalence case and, 67
Intellectualism, Orthodox Judaism and, 35–37
Interpersonal relationships, Orthodox Judaism, 157–158
Irrationality, religion and, xiv

Resistance
  ambivalence case, 49–52, 55
  born-again case, 102–106, 109
  feminist case, 128–131
  masochism case
    silence as, 76–78
    termination and, 76–78
Ritual
  defiance of, masochism case,
    90
  family dynamics and, 160–161
  feminist case, 138–139
  Orthodox Judaism and, 20–23
  psychological significance of, 5
  spontaneity and, 94
Roof, W. C., 149
Rosen, B., 21
Rubenstein, R., 5, 23, 26, 27

Sadism, born-again case, 114
Self-esteem
  God and, 53
  Moses and, 4
Sexism
  career and, 127–128, 133
  feminist case and, 126. *See also*
    Feminist case
Sex role
  family dynamics and, 159–160
  God and, 89–90
  Orthodox Judaism and, 84,
    85–86
  rebbitzin role and, 74, 87
  resentment toward, 79–80
Sexuality. *See also* Marital
    relationship
  aggression, masochism case,
    85
  born-again case, 101, 105–106,
    107, 111, 112–115
  countertransference,
    masochism case, 82
  dream analysis and, 53–54
  erotic transference
    feminist case, 138

    masochism case, 81
  feminist case, 138–139
  homosexuality, latent,
    ambivalence case, 59–61
  marital relationship and, 46–47
  Orthodox Judaism, 88, 157–158
Siegel, R., 134
Silence, masochism case and,
    76–78
Sklare, M., 3, 154
Smith, J., xv, 6
Somatic symptoms
  born-again case, 101
  countertransference and, 75–76
  masochism case, 72–73, 74
Spilka, B., xv, 6
Spontaneity, ritual and, 94
Strean, H., 44, 48, 50, 52, 54, 58,
    59, 63, 78, 82, 99, 106, 123,
    133
Success orientation, Orthodox
    Judaism and, 37–38
Sullivan, H. S., 39, 45, 134
Superego
  family dynamics and, 159–160
  Freud and, 133
  Moses and, 4
  Orthodox Judaism and, 28–35

Teitelbaum, S., 133
Telushkin, J., 29
Termination
  ambivalence case, 67–68
  born-again case, 118–120
  feminist case, 141–143
  masochism case, 93–94
  Orthodox Judaism and,
    163–166
Therapeutic alliance, born-again
    case, 104
Therapeutic relationship
  analysand's religious doubts,
    64–65
  depression and, 50
  honeymoon phase and, 54